WE SPEAK FOR OURSELVES

"Watkins anchors his new collection of essays in the voices, language, everyday realities, and dreams of black citizens. . . . [He] offer[s] deep critiques of the elitism and respectability that directly and indirectly censor voices. . . . A strong offering that brings nuance and multiplicity to readers attempting to decipher the black male urban experience while uplifting the stories, visions, and love that incubated a rising star."

—*Kirkus Reviews*

"[Watkins] shines a light on the perspective of poor Black people whose stories are missing from contemporary writings on race."

—*Essence*

"Reading *We Speak for Ourselves*, I can't help but admire D. Watkins. He is not another elite voice for the voiceless. He is, this book is, an amplifier of low-income Black people who have their own voices and have no problem using them. He dares us to listen."

—Ibram X. Kendi, National Book Award–winning author of *Stamped from the Beginning: The Definitive History of Racist Ideas in America*

"In a time of blunt-bladed posturing and hyperbolized impact, *We Speak for Ourselves* is a sharp gash into the psyche of America. Written as a relentless slice of his own life, Watkins avoids pretense as he puts language to his jagged experiences, not to encourage voyeurism but instead to push people to grapple and wrestle with the real lives so many talking heads attempt to muzzle, then fictionalize. Watkins has come to remind us that everyone deserves the opportunity to speak for themselves. Everyone."

—Jason Reynolds, *New York Times* bestselling author
and National Book Award finalist,
Long Way Down

"*We Speak for Ourselves* is full of insight into the America that serves as grist for the American dream. Its pages are abundant with wisdom and wit, integrity and love, not to mention enough laughs for a stand-up comedy routine. Over and over again, I found myself saying 'yes, yes, he's right,' and I ultimately finished feeling inspired to do better, to be more. D. Watkins proves once again why he isn't just a writer of the people but a people's literary champ for the here, now, and tomorrow."

—Mitchell S. Jackson, author of *Survival Math:*
Notes on an All-American Family

"Watkins's latest work shows the black community is not a monolith. We are a diverse and proud community, trying to come to grips with who we are, and sometimes wearing a mask within our own brother and sisterhood."

—April Ryan, *Under Fire: Reporting from the*
Front Lines of the Trump White House

"*We Speak for Ourselves* is an ode to those black people who understand that the first place where so many of us honed our understandings of knotty U.S. racial politics was in an American city, or rural town, fashioned as a 'hood' in the public imagination. Watkins writes with a profound love for the black forgotten that will compel all who read his timely words to never forget the black people and places so many cultural critics and thought leaders disremember with ease."

—Darnell L. Moore, author of *No Ashes in the Fire: Coming of Age Black & Free in America*

WE SPEAK
FOR
OURSELVES

HOW
WOKE CULTURE
PROHIBITS PROGRESS

D. WATKINS

ATRIA PAPERBACK

New York • London • Toronto • Sydney • New Delhi

ATRIA PAPERBACK

An Imprint of Simon & Schuster, Inc.
1230 Avenue of the Americas
New York, NY 10020

First Atria Paperback edition February 2020

ATRIA PAPERBACK and colophon are trademarks of Simon & Schuster, Inc.

For information about special discounts for bulk purchases, please contact Simon &
Schuster Special Sales at 1-866-506-1949 or business@simonandschuster.com.

The Simon & Schuster Speakers Bureau can bring authors to your live event. For
more information, or to book an event, contact the Simon & Schuster Speakers
Bureau at 1-866-248-3049 or visit our website at www.simonspeakers.com.

Interior design by Silverglass

Manufactured in the United States of America

1 3 5 7 9 10 8 6 4 2

Library of Congress Cataloging-in-Publication Data is available.

ISBN 978-1-5011-8782-7
ISBN 978-1-5011-8783-4 (pbk)
ISBN 978-1-5011-8784-1 (ebook)

For Thelma "Famma" Gill, with love. I still hear you. Thank you for the foundation. And to my heart, Caron, may we use that same foundation to build a beautiful future.

One day I prayed to you and said if I ever blow, I'd let 'em know
The stakes, and exactly what takes place in the ghetto.
—Jay-Z, *Where I'm From* (1997)

In the end, we will remember not the words of our enemies,
but the silence of our friends.
—Dr. Martin Luther King Jr., "The Trumpet of Conscience" (1967)

CONT

ENTS

A SEAT AT THE TABLE

Did you know there are different types of black people?

"Hello, young man," a scholarly, Danny Glover–looking guy laced in tweed said. "Are you enjoying yourself?"

"Yes, sir, this is a nice function."

He slowly looked me up and down. I cleaned up well—in my opinion anyway—but I did look out of place. You can really tell the difference between those three-thousand-dollar tailored suits and my cheap, thin H&M getup. I swear, if I made one wrong move, the pants and jacket would split in half. The people here dressed as if they attended galas for a living. Every person was cleaner than the next. Silk, sheer pocket squares, printed bow ties, sparkly accessories, and pointy little shoes could be seen in every direction, sliding across the gleaming marble floor. Multiple planet-sized chandeliers hung above us as tuxedoed servers offered crab balls, cucumber sandwiches, and some other hors d'oeuvres.

"What is your name, young man?"

"D.—I'm sorry, Dwight Watkins, sir."

"Ooh, okay!" he replied with a Kool-Aid smile, tilting his small oval frames to get a better look.

"Watkins as in Watkins Ice?"

"No."

"Watkins as in Watkins Security?"

"No, no." I laughed.

"So, what does your family do? What is your line of work?"

I told him I was in between jobs and my family worked at the places that hired them.

He frowned at me. All his nonverbal cues clearly said I wasn't the guy that he wanted to be talking to. Before I could get his name, he was already off meeting and greeting other guests.

✳

I never knew there was a black elite until I was at an event for the black elite. We all know about rich black people like Oprah, Jay-Z, and Diddy, but they're celebs. I'm talking about a wealthy class of non-famous African Americans who own art galleries, development companies, law firms, and medical practices. Jobs that I didn't really see when I was coming up.

"This event seems really nice," my friend Tia told me without blinking as we entered. "It's the kind of place you need to be."

I am a back-alley-block-party, dinner-and-salad-fork-are-the-same type of guy, but I'm also a good sport who is willing to hobnob with the dress-shoe crowd. Tia would always tell me about her new elite friends and about their parents being doctors, lawyers, architects, or the famous first black something in whatever field. She was constantly impressed by them—their stories expanded her perspective and ultimately mine as I listened, trying to figure out a way to understand this world. The idea of black journalists, photographers, and legal millionaires who didn't hoop or rap was foreign.

Before heading to the event, I almost choked myself out trying to learn how to tie a tie from a tutorial on YouTube—dude in the video talked way too fast and it sounded like he had hot food in his mouth. I wrapped the tie around my neck as if I was going to fix it before deciding to leave it in the car.

Tia's artsy friend noticed us as soon as we entered and tugged her arm to make a few introductions. "I'll be back. You are okay, right?" she said as they drifted off. I nodded my head.

"Can I get a double vodka with a splash of any type of juice?" I said to the bartender. "Just enough juice to change the color. Thank you, bro."

"No need to thank me, broooo, we are not mixing drinks," he smugly replied, looking me up and down and up again before pointing to a menu.

"You have to order off of this fixed list, thank you." I didn't trip, even though they had all the ingredients sitting out—I was determined to not be that guy. So I ordered off the menu, left a tip, and looked for a wall to hold up but instead encountered the tweed-Danny-Glover guy.

When Tia and her friend made their way back over to me, I jokingly told them about the exchange. Her friend told us that the Danny Glover look-alike was a professor who gives commentary on race, poverty, and surviving as a person of color in America. A race and poverty commentator with nothing to say to an unemployed black man, go figure.

I have since seen him appear on TV shows after a couple of killings of unarmed black males. He shared the same not-all-cops-are-bad-so-strategic-protest-will-equal-reform   perspective that dominates mainstream thought on the black experience and appears on the pages of the thousands of race books that drop every month.

Don't get me wrong, I'm excited about the number of race books flooding the publishing industry. We have an endless collection of black narratives, letters to racist and nonracist white people, and sensitive stories with the goal of making everyone feel safe enough to discuss America's problem with people of color. Contemporary black writers are hard at work defining the systemic issues that plague the African American experience, while our white counterparts are doing the same—swooping in as super-allies, schooling their lost friends on what it means to be black, and offering step-by-step lessons on acknowledging their own privilege. These projects are cool, but what happens once we finish reading all of the books on race in America?

Even if a person decides to apply action to the content that they read, there's another problem. Many of these books are missing the point. In fact, the authors of these books are among a huge tradition of thought leaders who missed the point, which explains why things never really change for most poor black people in America. These thought leaders define the black experience from a drone-like perspective—they have all the insight but strangely no connection to the black people they claim they are fighting for. The primary reason is that their books and language never include the very people who live the poor black experience every day.

I am talking about the experience of the black kids who are fighting to survive, the mothers and grandmothers who are holding families together, the men and women reentering society from incarceration—and what America has to offer other than the same hurdles it places in front of them. Hurdles such as poor housing, underfunded schools, and other social constraints that push young people into jail. The prison-industrial complex would not exist without failed policing strategies, lack of opportunity, and how black skin always seems to equal guilty in courtrooms across the country.

It is great that my people are trending on social media, cable news, and, well, maybe even in society. Still, in the midst of all the black narratives stacked on bookshelves, we have a problem—a major problem. People from the street are absent from them.

***

As I write this book, I've now been in and around the publishing world for four years. But I've been in the streets my whole life, which gives me a unique perspective. See, I'm not rich enough to be disconnected from my roots, but I'm just popular enough to get a few invites to private parties and events with top black thinkers, celebrity protesters (yes, this is a real thing), and the rest of the mouthpieces for the contemporary black experience in America. What I have observed from these functions is that many of the people who attend have something in common—they don't know or really associate with black people who aren't famous, social media celebrities, or from some type of fifty-generation Morehouse or Spelman family unless there is a camera crew around. Hence the lopsided selection of narratives we find.

I have nothing against anyone who has found success. However, many of these narratives don't tie into a big part of the black experience in this country, which is wrong on an extremely profound level.

Every time I hit these events or crack open a book about race, I encounter the fearful Black Nerd, which is normally a scared, thin, wiry, bookish kid who had to find a special route to school to avoid gang activity. Of course, they outsmart the thugs. Next, they grow up to become successful only to oppress poor blacks who come from the same place as the gang members they once avoided. All the while, they write books about what it means to be black and oppressed. I witnessed so many people advocate for Freddie Gray, the unarmed black man from Baltimore killed in police custody, but shun black kids from his neighborhood every day.

When I get a chance to catch up with some of the influencers and thought leaders, I ask them about that fear and then explain to them how their fear is a luxury that many of us will never enjoy.

To craft a gang-free route to school out of fear is a luxury.

What if you can't cut around the bad neighborhood because you live right in the center of it? In my neighborhood of East Baltimore, the devil knocked every day. Growing up, I couldn't avoid the violence because it was in my apartment, or across the hall, or on my block. Every road was paved with roses and thorns. You could have great experiences with amazing people, but you could also get your head cracked along the way, and that's how it is. The perspective of black people who know this but did not make it to college, to the boardroom, or out of public housing is often missed when these intellectuals attempt to define a contemporary black experience that is unfamiliar to them.

Many of my friends and I carry bullet fragments that click around in our joints when we walk. Our scars are badges of resiliency that we flash for any and every reason. I've had my head cracked. I've cracked the heads of others. Drugs have impacted everyone around my life, whether it was selling them, coping with addiction to them, or losing a family member or friend because of them.

All the while, in the midst of all the pain, many of us still share in the love of our family and community. Yes, family love does exist in low-income neighborhoods, although you wouldn't know it because that narrative gets left out as our current elite class of mouthpieces rely on '90s rap lyrics and censored BET movies to get their hood stories.

It's time for some of these so-called thought leaders and black experts to fall back. I'm not knocking them for their attempts to interpret the poor black experience, just like I don't judge the white liberal types who tackle me after book events so they can show me pictures of the black baby they just adopted. "D.! They said we can name him whatever we want since he's so young! So we are calling him Marcus, like Garvey!" (Yeah, this really happened, three times.)

Those people dibble and dabble in a world in which people like me are surviving. So, when I tell you that I just split a chicken box (four wings and fries with salt, pepper, ketchup, and hot sauce) with my homie Cook two weeks ago over in the Latrobe housing projects, and that he had never even heard of Black Lives Matter until I introduced him to it, you shouldn't be surprised because the protest movement is not a universal black experience, especially when you are just trying to survive the day-to-day.

Cook laughed and responded, "Why they rallyin' to change a white system that work perfect for whites in a white country for? Good luck with that!" And, you can't look at him like he's crazy, because that's just an assessment based on his experience. He reflects a common perspective among people like me, from the bottom, and you wouldn't know because we normally don't get invites to ivory tower galas and dress-shoe functions.

PART 1

DOWN BOTTOM

1

WHERE I COME FROM

The homies and I like to sit around and brag about who had it worse—you know, who was the poorest, who went to the dirtiest school, and who came the closest to being murdered the most times. This is fun for us. You might hear one of us say "Walking to school on top of piles of broken glass and drug needles with busted shoes is a luxury, man! I had to walk to school on all of that without feet!" Of course, we all have feet. The conversations serve as a way for us to acknowledge our resiliency.

There is a lot of truth in our jokes. In fact, you might think of the jokes as a coping mechanism for dealing with hard truths. Some of us had it worse than others. People who are aware of our backstory always ask the same question, "How'd you make it out?" The answer is simple: *luck*.

Luck is the one thing that bonds us. It's why I'm now a writer, why my friend Tony instructs free fitness trainings, and why my cousin Kevin works with kids. We are all from the street, but we were fortunate enough to avoid being murdered or getting locked up for fifty years for a crime we didn't commit. Well, there's still a chance for these things to happen. We still live in Baltimore.

I'm from the east side of town—my neighborhood is called DDH, short for Down Da Hill, or what many of us call Down Bottom. The row homes in my neighborhood cascade downward on a series of sloping hills. Like most of East Baltimore, or Baltimore in general, every family isn't poor or soaring below the poverty line, but the drug trade has affected us all, creating many different realities.

Some of us fell while others were able to fly.

✻

THIS IS HOW IT WORKS...

My A1 from day one was Hurk, Wop seen it all, and I crushed on Nay.

Hurk's mother was a junkie. His father, we don't know. Fathers were rare back when we were growing up. His living situation was always dysfunctional and kids around our neighborhood reminded him about it daily: "Ya mova smoke crack!" "You ain't got no daddy!" "You dirty!" And so on. Hurk's shoes would bust at the seams where the string unraveled. His clothes stunk. It wasn't because the homie was dirty, he just didn't have running water in his house. To add insult to injury, we would see his mom begging for change, digging in the trash, or following strange guys into an alley.

Wop, *the big fella*, was the first to grow a mustache and wear a size eleven shoe when we could loosely fit size sevens. He was a man-child, husky enough to play sports two grades up. At ten he smacked the wind out of twelve-year-old boys on the football field. On the basketball court, he could drop his shoulder in the paint and knock an older kid on his back as he took two steps into an easy layup. When we were on the court, Wop's pop, Big Wop, would be our pretend coach, giving us plays to run and exercises to do in between his crack sales.

I like open shots. I can hit an open three-pointer from

anywhere—half-court, the gym door, the locker, the parking lot, maybe even Texas. Put a rim in East Baltimore and place me in Houston, and if I'm open, it's going down, baby. Nothing but net. That's a joke. I do really like open shots—but when Nay watched, I forced it. Nay was the prettiest girl in East Baltimore. She was the ghetto Rudy Huxtable. Art in motion. God's greatest accomplishment wrapped in an eleven-year-old-girl's body. I was ten at the time, but I was ready for her. She and her friends would walk by the park while we hooped, and she'd scream through the gate, "Y'all can't play no ball!" I'd look, acting like I wasn't looking, throw sixty crossovers, take unauthorized shots, up and under three defenders. I'd go head up with Wop's grown-man-sized left shoulder, slapping the pavement and popping back up in milliseconds, yelling "I'm aight, keep playin'!" When I scored, I always glanced at her for approval, praying she noticed. "Aye lover boy!" Big Wop would yell at me. "Pay attention! Keep your head in the game!"

Hurk was stick boney but better than us all. Holey shoes or not, it didn't matter—his lanky frame would weave seamlessly in between defenders. He was the first to use the crossover effectively, dropping anyone who dared to play defense; the first to slap the backboard; and definitely the first to dunk. His little brother, Tay—three years our junior—was slated to be better; he was always selected before at least six older kids in a ten-man pickup game and no one really wanted to guard him. He would run you breathless on the court and had one of the best midrange jump shots we'd ever seen.

Guns banged every night, and crowds always form after the smoke clears. One night red-and-blue lights danced on my bedroom window, across the street sign, and on our basketball court. I went outside to join the crowd. The court was starting to overflow as the medics rushed in and plainclothes cops draped warning tape around the scene. Nay was standing alone by the gate.

"Hey, Nay, what happened?" I asked. She squeezed me tight and said, "Big Wop, Big Wop." Big Wop was DOA; lost his life on the court he loved so much. None of us knew what to say to Wop. People always say, "Everything is going to be okay." But is it ever really okay? Young black people get murdered all the time and some praying grandma always says, "It'll be better on the other side." But is it really?

Tay made the basketball team over at Oliver Recreation Center, but the coach yelled at him until he didn't want to play anymore. His teachers yelled at him until he didn't want to go to school anymore. He still played pickup ball, but we all yelled at him because he'd ask us to repeat things nine or ten times— we even started calling him Def Tay. Tay didn't have a hearing problem. Hurk said some type of insect planted eggs inside Tay's eardrum.

Even when Hurk's mom lost custody of all her kids, they still hung around the neighborhood—Hurk eventually grew tired of the hand-me-downs and sob stories so he started slanging crack.

By high school, Nay looked ready for *Vogue*. Slicked baby hair pulled back into soft pigtails and barrettes transformed into bouncy wraps that covered her left eye like Aaliyah's—the kind that older women wore. The little Air Jordans at the end of her bowed legs were trendy high heels now. By this time, she had a real Gucci clutch while other girls had fake ones. At ten years old, I didn't have a shot with her, but there was hope. By fourteen, she was completely out of my league. Older dudes with Acuras and BMWs would drop her off at school. They were the hustlers.

Hurk paid $40 for his fitted cap, $450 for his gold teeth, $1,000 for his Cuban link, $900 for the diamond-cut Virgin Mary charm that dangled from it, $300 for his Coogi sweater, $600 for his white Pelle Pelle leather jacket, $90 for his Guess jeans, and $150 for his Nikes. He would wear all that to the basketball court. "It's nothing!" he yelled. "I'm never wearing this again, who need a coat?" I hated that he hustled but loved to see him shine.

Hurk would often clown me for not getting close to Nay. I'd ignore the jokes, and Hurk would say, "You'll never get her, she only like dudes from West Baltimore. They spend that cash!" Wop would laugh and guzzle his drink. It was usually gin, sometimes Hennessy, but mostly gin. By high school, he was drinking heavily—always telling stories about how he would've been balling at a top private school if his dad were alive.

I struggled through high school but had to finish because I wanted to go to college. Hurk was making a lot of money, so for him, there was no need for school. Tay followed in Hurk's footsteps, throwing his basketball dreams away and blending in with the older kids on the corner just like he did on the court.

"I need some money, Hurk," Wop said one day. "Show me how to do it, yo, please." I tried to get Wop to hoop with me in a league, but he was in the streets now too. Hurk had him selling loose pills, and Wop messed the money up over and over again. "You need to go back to school up at Patterson," Hurk laughed. "You can't add, fat boy!" He took Wop off the money and made him the lookout before he eventually graduated to muscle. Whenever the opportunity presented itself, Wop was laying an aluminum bat across somebody's skull. Then they started playing with pistols.

By tenth grade, Nay was pregnant by one of those West Baltimore dudes. The child's father never came around to meet his daughter, but another hustler picked up the pieces. She had her second kid before the twelfth grade. Her new baby's father was a baller too. He didn't just drop her off in luxury cars, he bought her one. A white beamer with a light tint and a sunroof. She picked me up in it when we went to Wop's funeral. Yeah, Wop went out just like his dad, gunned down a few blocks away from where his father passed.

I vowed to never sell drugs. Wop, like many of the dudes from Down Bottom, had wanted to go to college. Even though his dreams faded after his dad passed, he still had moments when he would tell me, "I'ma leave this corner and head off to college, bro, watch. I'ma be a big, UConn two-guard, watch!"

I enrolled in college and dropped out about two months later—ended up back on the block and even hustled with Hurk. We ran the streets slanging dope like it was legal. "I can't deal with street guys anymore," Nay told me after her second child's father caught thirty years. "My mom is going to watch these kids. I'm getting a nursing degree and a good churchgoing college husband. One that wears church shoes every day, even on Tuesdays." She stood over me frantically clapping. "One that wears church shoes from Sunday to Sunday!"

I wasn't thinking about church or college, just money. Hurk was too—so much so that he ended up stealing from all of our friends, getting two of them shot, and almost getting me killed in the process. The dollar trumped the jokes, the laughs, the lost friends, the memories, and everything else. Dude banged his pistol in every section of East Baltimore all the way up until the cops grabbed him. They snatched up Tay too. Some younger dudes took his spot and the cycle continued.

You couldn't mentor teens like us, who drove a new Lexus, unless you pushed a Bentley. However, Bentley owners didn't drive through my section of East Baltimore, and if they did, the driver wasn't hopping out and telling my friends and me to stay away from drugs.

Growing up we never listened to anyone positive, only the guys who hustled and showed us the rewards—the celebrity treatment, the money, the cars, and the clothes. Their advice made sense, so we took it and captured neighborhoods—we flashed pistols, drained property values, and pedaled poison. Some of us got caught and copped out to dozens of years, but we kept going. The money didn't stop, so why would we? Some of us took bullets and came back to work. Some of us died. Still, after the funerals let out and the repast was over, we kept going. We never stopped.

✳

Everybody in Down Bottom loved Snaggletooth Rib with the big gold tooth and the one heavy eyebrow that used to slang with us. He was the comeback king. Crack a joke on him and he had four ready to go for you. They were good ones too, the kind that put your insecurities out in the open for everyone to see. Rib probably would have toured the world as a famous stand-up comedian if we knew careers like that were obtainable. We didn't.

One hot day, Rib plus about fifteen of us hung our heads deep in a dice game. Rib being himself was clowning the winners and losers, shuffling cash, and working the circle.

"Bet the twenty, bet the fifty," he'd yell. "And I got one-dollar bets for the rest of you clowns, cuz y'all smell like poverty!"

A few more guys joined the game. One of them pushed a wobbly stroller. He parked it and laid some money down, which he quickly lost. A baby peeked out and squeaked a little. Dude said, "Hold up, son-son, I be right back."

"Yo, you leaving your son to gamble wit us?" Rib laughed, pointing at the dude. "You gotta be top three worst fathers in the world! Raise y'all kids right! Y'all dummies don't be like this dummy!"

"You always think everything funny, ha ha," the dude barked back at Rib, pulling the stroller closer to his person. "You funny, right, Rib?"

"Shut up and keep losing your baby food money! Y'all both on the titty milk diet tonight." Rib chuckled with a face-wide grin. You could see the rest of us laughing in the reflection on his big gold tooth.

Right there, the dude whipped an arm-sized gun out of the stroller and unleashed a parade of shots into Rib, spun around, then aimed it at the rest of us before snatching every dollar off of the ground. Rib died at the scene. We scattered and came back a few hours later to build a hood memorial of empty Hennessy bottles, teddy bears, and the "I Love You" balloons that the ladies liked to tape to the poles. We sang Tupac's "Life Goes On." We drank. We mourned. We wore RIP T-shirts with Rib's face on the front and back. And soon enough, we were all back gambling, right back to hustling. Red tops, blue tops, yellow tops, five-, six-, ten-, twenty-, and fifty-dollar vials. We stayed open all day, right over the spot where Rib's blood had dried.

That type of instant trauma should've forced us to change our ways, leave the game, and truly honor our fallen friend, but we

didn't. We could've been nicer people, but we weren't. After a few
other friends fell, I could've learned to value life more.

Of course, we called each other family, but we didn't act like
it. Everybody celebrated the wins and quickly blamed each other
for the losses; like narcissists we never took personal responsibility
for anything that went wrong. Guns were flashed, safeties clicked
off, and pointed at each other during every disagreement. The
stories of Rib, Hurk, Wop, and dozens more make up the bulk of
my life. I've been on the wrong side of the pistol plenty of times.

I once heard a black cop on a community engagement panel
say, "These kids are so dumb, they just idolize stupid drug dealers! What's wrong with them?"

The answer is *nothing*. There is nothing wrong with kids who
are subject to a reality that has mirrored my own. The kids aren't
dumb. Nobody dreams of breaking the law or looking up to killers and dealers. The street hustler mentality is handed down to
you—it becomes a tradition, you inherit it.

In neighborhoods like Down Bottom, where few people can
afford to leave, the hustlers have the monopoly on appeal; they
got the juice. They are the most affluent people around, have the
nicest things, and are always present. None of us dream of being
affiliated with these hustlers or the drug trade. It just happens.
And it goes like this for so many kids. Not just in Baltimore, but
all over the country.

※✲※

My years in the streets might present some of the reasons why I
may not be qualified to preach on blackness, critique activism,
or have any say on how these things work. I'm from the bottom.
I'm as flawed as anyone else, maybe even more. I've done some

good. I left a life of crime. I went to college. All the while staying in my neighborhood in an effort to pull some people off the streets. I wrote a couple of books and hit the road, offering my story.

My words have inspired some. Others, I'm sure, have been repulsed by them. I am not special, or gifted, or chosen to lead the Negro nation.

I'm just a regular guy, a voice in the middle of a sea of voices that don't seem to matter to most—which is why we may forever be misrepresented unless we speak for ourselves.

2

JUST PASS THE MIC

Representation is everything. Who gets to speak for whom?

Every time I turn around, I see some pundit or politician on TV defining the black experience in America, selecting our leaders, or overgeneralizing us—acting like our shared skin color equals identical feelings. It needs to stop.

Let me give you an example of what poor representation looks like.

In the summer of 2017 in Charlottesville, Virginia, white racists, dressed in boot-cut khaki pants and off-brand polo shirts and armed with tiki torches, marched in the Unite the Right rally, protesting the proposed removal of the Confederate statue of Robert E. Lee from Emancipation Park. The bulk of the crowd probably didn't know anything about Lee, they just wanted to be part of something racist. As counterprotesters confronted the racists, conflict ensued. Nineteen people were seriously injured; Heather Heyer, a thirty-two-year-old woman, was killed after being struck by a car driven by an evil racist.

From my couch, I watched a few media outlets cover the story and was shocked by the idea of white men complaining about not getting a fair shake in America. White men are probably the only people in this country who can wave pistols at police officers, live to tell the story, and not spend the rest of their lives in prison even if they are convicted.

Liberal-leaning news outlets were furious at the events that unfolded in Charlottesville that day, while Fox News—yes, I watch Fox News for comical purposes only—took a softer approach to condemning the white nationalists' actions. However, I wasn't as offended by Fox News's coverage or the marching racists nearly as much as I was by some of the black pundits who offered their take on the events.

These guys sat on television and cried because a race rally took place in America.

Let me be clear, I'm aware that African Americans didn't create racism, slavery, or the infrastructure that serves to oppress whole groups of people; however, I can't believe this Charlottesville demonstration made two TV pundits, both grown black men, cry. As far as I could tell, they weren't crying over the death of Heather Heyer. I would've understood that, no one deserves to die, especially a person fighting against white supremacy. It seemed as though they were disappointed that America is a place where racist rallies take place. I wondered what kind of America they were living in where whites proudly hating black people was surprising. The tears of those two pundits left me with one question: Do they even know any black people?

I Googled both men and couldn't find evidence of them shedding any public tears for Michael Brown, Trayvon Martin, Sandra Bland, or Tamir Rice. With all the race-based tragedies in America over the past few years—from the modern-day lynching of Eric Garner to Walter Scott being shot in the back—these two brothers chose to cry over an underattended, uninspiring, race rally. Please!

If it were two random dudes crying, I wouldn't care. However, these are the guys brought on television for their black perspective. They get to speak as representatives for black America and that's a serious problem. I asked a few friends, black people who know we are somewhere near the bottom of the American food chain, about the crying and they laughed at the idea. Laughed so much that they almost cried at those guys shedding tears over a rally like the one in Charlottesville. We confront racism every day, on the job if we get hired, definitely from the cops, and from the annoying clerks who follow us from the front to the back of the store, just to make sure we aren't stealing.

I'm from the bottom, and what I mean by bottom is the first-generation scholars, the project babies, the people without Wi-Fi, the workers, the people most likely to get hit by police bullets. We are the subjects of protests, the rarely heard from even as our deaths are debated by media personalities who wouldn't step foot on our blocks. I don't attempt to speak for everyone—but those guys don't represent us. We'll cry over the lack of gainful employment, the fear of our kids being harassed by cops, our loved ones being murdered, but definitely, definitely not over a racist rally. And if you knew us, you'd know that.

To quote the brilliant scholar and activist Dr. Su'ad Abdul Khabeer, "You don't need to be a voice for the voiceless. Just pass the mic."

3

THE HURDLES

Imagine being fast, really fast, so fast that you are invited to compete in races. You always go, and you always win. Even when you stayed up all night drinking and get off to a slow start, or when your ankle hurts, or when you don't feel like running at all, you still win. You always close strong, the head of the pack, everyone knows your skill.

Imagine your talent taking you to the next level. Getting you into competition after competition, with all of them ending the same—you crossing the finish line first. So one day, you're asked to compete in a race with a person who is twenty times slower than you. You know this because you've beat him ten times already. Let's call him Ron. Ron's sloppy and out of shape, with short legs and two left feet. You are tall, lean, and built like an action figure. You are a professional athlete. The purse is $20,000, and there's no prize for second place, except honorable mention once a year in February.

You are set to race Ron but there's a catch. You have to run blindfolded. You don't care: you've beat Ron ten times, you know the track, you know it's a straight shot with no curves, and you can dust him in seconds, break the FINISH tape, and remove the blindfold for an easy $20,000.

So, you and Ron take your positions. A person walks out with a black blindfold and wraps it tight around your head. Once the blindfold is secured, the same person places ten hurdles on your side of the track.

"On your mark, get set, go!"

The pistol screams POW!

You both take off. Who do you think will win the race?

❋

In an effort to critique the system, and change it even, we must acknowledge what happens to its products. I'd hate to go too far without acknowledging the many hurdles that may come with being black in America. So, let's get some of these out of the way.

- **Schools:** Your school will probably lack the necessary technology you need to be competitive in the digital world. Here's how the former mayor of Baltimore Martin O'Malley allocated funds during his tenure, as found by the *Baltimore Sun*:

YEAR	SCHOOLS	POLICE
2000	$200.3 million	$231.4 million
2001	200.8 "	252.5 "
2002	200.8 "	273.9 "
2003	200.9 "	303.4 "
2004	201.2 "	295.4 "
2005	207.6 "	315.0 "
2006	207.8 "	325.7 "
2007	207.9 "	347.0 "

- **Cops:** Those cops that received a hefty amount of that O'Malley funding will proudly beat you senseless at some point. They're more crooked than the crooks.
- **Food Deserts:** Fried food drenched in salt is available on every corner in the neighborhood. Sometimes you'll have to travel miles to find an apple, and then more miles to see a non-GMO apple the size of a basketball.
- **Poor Housing:** "I'll fix your heat if you give me a piece" can sometimes be heard in the halls of public housing. The maintenance men who service the residents in the projects weren't doing their jobs unless tenants had sex with them.
- **Drug Trade:** Open-air drug markets are real and they affect everyone in the community. Drugs will play a part in your life. The drug world also comes with guns, jail, and death.
- **Poverty:** Payday loan businesses always say "yes" when banks say "no." The loan clerks laugh as their interest rates strangle you.
- **Black Taxes:** You will always have to work harder than white folk in order to have the same opportunities. And if you do make it out, this black skin of yours will literally cost you for showing up at places you are undesired.

The "Black Tax" is a term my friends and I jokingly throw around from time to time. It basically means that African Americans have to work ten times as hard as white people to get the same things. The Black Tax is very real. A good example would be the fact that Angela Bassett, who gave us Tina Turner, Betty X, Notorious B.I.G.'s mom Voletta Wallace, and Ramonda in *Black Panther*, doesn't have an Academy Award, but Ben Affleck has two!

Look at the last two presidents. Imagine if Barack Obama had said women should be grabbed by the p***y, lusted over or flirted with the idea of dating his own daughters, refused to share his tax returns, trashed his staffers on Twitter, skipped reading his presidential briefings, was accused of cheating with a porn star and having his attorney pay her off while Michelle was pregnant, and called Meryl Streep overrated, all while being a black guy in office.

"Barack who?" is probably what we would all be saying right now. Obama had to be beyond squeaky clean to become and stay president for eight years. Everything was perfect about the dude, from his credit to his teeth.

"Only in this country!" various Uncle Toms have said to me over the years. "Any hardworking person can achieve whatever they want." Next, they start talking about bootstraps.

The problem with the people who go off on those respectability tirades is their inability to imagine another person's situation. They are grossly shortsighted, only able to see their own success and to use it as a measure when judging others, no matter where that other person comes from.

It's a failure to fully appreciate history to repeat the platitude "Slavery was so long ago!," when the Emancipation Proclamation was issued a mere 155 years ago. If you count the punitive, crippling effects of the Black Codes and Jim Crow laws, sharecropping ("slavery by another name") and indentured servitude, and the "war on drugs" and the "prison-industrial complex," blacks have been enslaved in this land for about four hundred years.

After slavery came the Black Codes, a set of laws passed in many southern states during 1865 and 1866 that placed limitations on black freedom. Some of the laws prohibited black people from owning firearms, voting, gathering in groups of worship, and learning to read and write. Blacks then suffered from the separate-but-equal Jim Crow laws that dominated until the Civil Rights Act was passed in 1964.

In theory, this all sounds like old news. We did elect that black president with the perfect teeth, and he served two terms, which means that equality is finally real, right? Wrong. The country elected an openly racist president who assembled a staff that is either outright racist or turns a blind eye to racists. Chief economic advisor Larry Kudlow hosted a publisher of white nationalist literature at an event, and Darren Beattie, a Trump speechwriter, resigned after news surfaced that he had attended a conference for white nationalists. Someone painted "NIGGER" on LeBron James's Los Angeles property; someone painted "Kill Niggers" on the African Burial Ground Monument, which has been described as "a sacred space in Manhattan" by the National Park Service; and a white employee in Philadelphia's U.S. Mint building placed a noose in a black employee's work station.

And let's not forget about Rashon Nelson and Donte Robinson, who were waiting for a friend in a Philadelphia Starbucks before they ordered, and the store manager called the police on them. They were arrested for trespassing. How do you get arrested for trespassing in a public place? That's a Black Tax.

These stories happen over and over again and, unfortunately, not enough of them go viral. I honestly believe that the ability to spread these incidents far and wide via social media is one of our best remedies at the moment. It's not foolproof, but it's a great tool and a step in the right direction.

I recently sat alone at the bar of a restaurant across the street from where I work. A nervous server made me two horrible mixed drinks. I didn't complain, I just watched the Cavs game and waited for my ride. The melted ice made the second drink taste a little better.

"Can I get my check please?" I asked. She nodded, but then ran off to wait on another table.

"D., how you doing, my man?" said a square-faced guy in a baggy sweat suit as he approached me. "It's been a long minute since the last time I saw you!"

I had no idea who he was. I just smiled and said, "Wassup, champ?"

He flopped on a stool two chairs down from mine, screamed out his order, and started spilling everything to me—his jobs, his baby mothers, his record label, and the secret business that he wasn't ready to let me in on. Dude had the timing and facial expressions of a seasoned stand-up comedian. I couldn't stop laughing, but it was time for me to go.

The waitress came back and filled his drink order. "Can I get my check, please?" I asked again. "I gotta roll."

She walked over with the leather booklet, I extended my arm, and she bypassed it, placing the bill on the table. I didn't complain; some don't like to directly hand other people objects. I looked at the bill. Not only had she put the food and drink ordered by this dude who I barely knew on my tab, but she'd included an 18 percent gratuity.

"Um, excuse me," I said, waving in her direction. "I didn't come here with this guy. Why is his stuff on my bill? He didn't even get his food yet."

"Oh, I saw you talking to him." She blushed. "I thought you guys were a party."

"But he's like two stools down," I said. "Anyway, what's this 18 percent gratuity about?"

"That's our new policy," she pleaded. "I don't want to do it, but I have to."

I didn't believe a word this lady said, but she saved me some money. Her added tip was six dollars, when I probably would've slipped her ten.

I asked the other guys at work about a new included gratuity policy, and of course none of them had heard of it. They are white. I am black. That is a real-life tax.

✳

That's the game. That's your race and these are your hurdles. The problem is so many of us grow up in this *other* America thinking it's normal to watch generation after generation fall victim to the same traps that are nearly impossible to escape.

Experiencing success in America as a black person from a poor neighborhood is like running through rush-hour traffic in New York and not being hit by a car. Success is impossible if you can't jump these hurdles, but first, you must know they exist.

4

THE TRADITION
OF FAILURE

What do you do for a living?

Let's just say you are an accountant. Now, imagine crunching numbers inside of a walk-in freezer. Would you be as effective? This is what's expected of the students in the Baltimore City Public School System.

While scrolling Instagram, I came across some photos of students and teachers with their coats on indoors. They weren't about to go on a field trip. They were trying to learn. More images and videos surfaced where students and teachers alike sat wrapped in blankets, balled up, freezing with cold puffs coming out of their mouths as they rubbed their hands together, trying to get through the day. Mind you, this is 2018. No heat in a public school in the most powerful nation in the world . . . in 2018.

Well, they say a picture is worth a thousand words. Let me tell you what some of those words said to me: Elected officials don't care about black children. The lack of progress made in public schools over the last fifty years is embarrassing and anyone who has the power to fix this but chooses not to truly wants poor black kids to fail.

The education hierarchy in this country is historic. During slavery, African servants spent countless days cooking, cleaning, being raped and beaten, sweating in the fields, and occasionally being lynched, while the children of their rich white masters were being educated. The 1800s saw schools pop up all over the United States, and by the end of the nineteenth century, free public education was available for all white children. Blacks have been in America since 1619 and received virtually no schooling until after President Abraham Lincoln issued the Emancipation Proclamation in 1863. That is a 244-year head start given to whites—244 years of exposure to scientific reasoning and philosophical thought, hundreds of years to discover the power of books and reading and shape dreams into reality.

The Lincoln administration made a conscious effort to right the wrongs in education along with other social injustices through the Freedmen's Bureau, established in 1865. Charged with clothing, feeding, employing, and otherwise helping newly freed blacks become US citizens, it even had dispensation to grant land. The Reconstruction era in the United States, those couple of years when the South was to rebuild itself from 1865 through 1867, would have been a great time to help blacks assimilate to the dominant culture through education. For the first time, the United States was seeing the rise of black business owners, black politicians, and the black church, but our country didn't capitalize on that opportunity. None of that success led to a rise in black schools.

Lincoln's promises died with him that night at the theater in 1865. Andrew Johnson, the next president, vetoed the Freedmen's Bureau's renewal in 1866. He confiscated the land African Americans had acquired in the South and gave it back to the white southerners who occupied it before the war. From 1866 to 1869, Johnson depleted the Freedmen's Bureau's funds, and it was eventually dismantled in full by his successor, Ulysses S. Grant, in 1872.

Sure, schools for freed slaves emerged. Within a year of emancipation, at least eight thousand former slaves began attending schools in Georgia; eight years later, those same black schools struggled to contain nearly twenty thousand students. Scores of children piled into these shacks, trying to compete while dealing with broken or no desks, leaky ceilings, and limited utensils. Sound familiar? Jim Crow laws allowing racial segregation guaranteed that the gap would widen as years passed. By the end of the nineteenth century, seventeen states and the District of Columbia required school segregation by law. Four others allowed the option.

That seemed poised to change when, in 1951, thirteen families from Topeka, Kansas, filed a lawsuit against their board of education. Like their ancestors, they wanted a quality education for their children—similar to what white children in the United States had been receiving for decades. The case came to be known as *Brown v. Board of Education* and was a major victory in the fight for education for black students. *Brown v. Board of Education* showed an immense amount of promise, giving many blacks hope that the United States could change. The landmark unanimous Supreme Court decision of 1954 overturned the *Plessy v. Ferguson* verdict of 1896, ruling that separate schools for blacks and whites were unconstitutional.

But the idea of blacks and whites being schooled together sent the nation into a frenzy. On June 11, 1963, George Wallace, governor of Alabama, went as far as to stand in the entrance to the University of Alabama, flanked by state troopers, so that black students couldn't get in to register, standing down only after President John F. Kennedy called in the National Guard.

"White flight" was the remedy for many Caucasians petrified by the thought that their child might share a classroom with a Negro. They took their tax money, their resources, and their high-quality schools with them to the burbs. Blockbusting, the practice of pushing down property values in a neighborhood through rumors of an imminent influx of some undesirable group, and redlining, the practice of denying and charging more for banking services in an effort to racially construct a neighborhood, were the most publicized means of keeping the races separate.

So there you have it: poor schools, institutionalized segregation, and minimal funding not only cultivated the deep roots of educational denial, but also strengthened the foundation upon which achievement gaps are built today. The combination of all of these historical events led to what I call the "Tradition of Failure." The Tradition was not self-imposed. Obviously, African Americans can take some personal responsibility for the state of our race; however, many of us do not know the root causes of these issues because we come from people who were forced to survive through the harsh realities these systems created, leading all the way back to the day our ancestors left Elmina, the former slave port in Ghana that launched us on our journey to this new world.

Our ancestors did not have a clue what was waiting for them on the other side of the Atlantic Ocean. Perhaps worse, we entered America as the lazy, ungrateful enemy without even knowing why, and it has been an uphill battle full of limitless racial and social restraints every step of the way. We didn't invent the idea of race or conceptualize the theory of free labor and what it could mean on a global scale. We just did what we were forced to do, and have been paying the price ever since.

Fast-forward to 2019, where it is hard enough for inner-city kids to learn with ancient, Columbus-praising textbooks that have zero cultural relevance—now imagine doing that in the blistering cold. Where's the reform?

Some parents have to work, and sending their kids to freezing schools is the only option. Many rely on school meals and need to make sure their children are cared for while they go out and look for the nonexistent jobs that Speaker of the House Paul Ryan says they don't want to do.

"Education is the key to making it out here! Stay in school!" is what some of the older dudes used to say back in the day, and they were partially right; but success depends on the quality of education you receive. Sitting in a school without heat, technology, or updated textbooks is like being given a car without wheels.

The kids of today need laptops to compete, but they don't even have simple things like heat and AC. A clean and comfortable learning environment equipped with technology is everything, and the lack has created generations of disadvantaged students, including myself.

I attended Baltimore public schools, and nothing has really changed since the days of Lincoln. My older siblings, parents, and everyone else have experienced the same thing. I don't know any black person from Baltimore who remembers schools *not* having a problem with the air, heat, and technology in general. As kids, we had to adjust to learning in the cold—it was a part of our reality—and as a result the bulk of my friends and I who actually graduated exited grossly unprepared.

Some kids learn to function in the worst environments, but they are the lucky ones. For others, the poor conditions leave them frustrated and uninspired. They look at their broken schools and their broken homes and then notice that the trap house has heat, video games, and you can actually make money. You really get paid on your first day of work.

Young dealers and killers aren't born that way. The collection of failed systems, like poorly maintained public schools, make them this way. I'm happy that we now have social media as a tool to share these failures with the masses. Airing out a city's dirty laundry should inspire them to clean it quicker, but whether they do remains to be seen.

Before passing judgment on our teachers, our young people, and the crime rate, remember that it was 2018 and we were still stuck in the 1800s.

5

TOO POOR FOR
POP CULTURE

"Hey mister, you're going up tonight. Good luck!" read an email from Sarah Hepola, the culture editor for Salon.com, back on February 4, 2014.

My literary agent, Barbara, and I had signed a contract for her to sell the rights to my debut memoir *The Cook Up* back in 2012. Two years later, we were still struggling to sell the book.

"Hey D.!" Barbara had said with excitement a few months back, "You should try to publish an essay in *Huffington Post* or *Salon*. That will help get your voice out there and make it easier for me to sell this book!"

I had never submitted to an online magazine—only local literary journals that no one read—so I did a little research and learned that getting pubbed by a digital news outlet wasn't difficult at all, you just had to pitch until they were tired of you. That night I wrote a piece explaining how my friends and I were so broke that we couldn't afford to keep up with pop culture. How can you tweet or know the latest trends without Wi-Fi?

My essay, titled "Too Poor for Pop Culture," went on to explain why access to information is class based. I closed the piece with a critique of Obama: How his presidency was extremely inspiring, but really didn't deliver us from anything. We didn't make any extra money and gunshots still banged outside of our front doors every night. I submitted it to *Huff Post*, who said they loved it but they needed me to cut it from two thousand to one thousand words. *Gawker* loved it too but didn't run it for whatever reason. Then Sarah from *Salon* not only loved it but also edited it and gave it a run date.

At the time, I was a flat-broke adjunct professor at Sojourner-Douglass College making $1,100 per class per semester, and at Coppin State University making $1,700 per class per semester. I taught five classes between both schools, which added up to about $390 per week before taxes. To make matters worse, we were paid in thirds. I had to wait weeks after the semester started to get that first installment and then stretch that check with the hopes of making it to my next round of payments.

In between check time, I did some substitute teaching when work was available, shot rap videos like a young Hype Williams, and built WordPress websites. I even filmed a funeral once. A dude called me up and asked how much I'd charge. I told him, "I don't do funerals, bro. Sorry." He said he had $600 for me, and I replied, "Should I wear all black?" I definitely could not afford to miss that, because after paying the mortgage, light, credit cards, and cell phone bills, I barely had enough money for anything else.

The low pay that came with being an adjunct professor didn't really bother me because I loved teaching more than sex and money. I would have done it for free. Books changed my life. I figured they could do the same for students who hated or thought they hated reading. I was dying to show students the transformative power of words by assigning relatable material like *Decoded* by Jay-Z and *The Coldest Winter Ever* by Sister Souljah. Sometimes reading was the only thing that kept my mind off the trauma that comes with being broke. Well, that and my own ambitions as a writer.

I wanted it all—bestsellers, tour dates, my own sneaker by Nike, and anything else that I thought came with making it as a writer. I thought I was close to achieving these things when I signed with my literary agent, Barbara, two years prior; however, things were not shaping up the way I wanted them to. Here I was an aspiring writer who shared cigarettes at Old Town Mall with other aspirants—the aspiring filmmakers, crack dealers, photographers, crackheads, 24-7 pill chasers, and everybody else who was always working toward something that was out of our reach. We were all about $125 away from having zero in our bank accounts—that is, if we had accounts at all.

I hit Sarah, the *Salon* editor, with a thank you, and made my way down to the mall to see who was out. Honestly, I wanted to ask her how long it was going to take to receive the $125 freelance check from *Salon*. But I didn't stress it. Everything was all good. This would be my first time appearing in a major publication. Suddenly, broke didn't feel so bad. The simplest things can numb the pain of poverty—selling an essay, that first exhale after taking a long pull from a Newport, or the moment your chest stops burning after taking a shot at the bar.

5:00 PM

I reached the mall around 5 PM. Vacant stores and active people lined the block. Young boys hit dope sales on both sides of the street as I parked by the alley and hopped out.

"Yo! Wassup? Y'all good? I love y'all."

"Luv you too, D. Watk!" they said. We squeezed hands and gave daps, hugs, and compliments over and over again—that's the ritual. We have to say "I love you" every time we see each other around here. Baltimore is a small town with a high murder rate and every day we see loved ones pass before their time.

"I heard you teaching, dummy!" said Mumbles with the heavy jaws, walking out of the barbershop. "My aunt said D. Watk wit the jughead is my professor and he good at it too! He funny. I said, 'Hell no! For real?'"

Mumbles is called "Mumbles" because he tries to speak at the speed his ideas develop, causing him to skip words and, well, mumble. Most of his family is from East Baltimore, just like mine. We met back when we were nine or ten.

"Yeah, bro, I teach. What class she in?" I laughed. "I think I know who your aunt is, cuz of y'all big jaws! Whole family look like Kanye after the car accident, dummy!"

Mumbles laughed. "I don't know the class, feel me, but keep doing your thing, champ! Only professor round here! I really thought you was gonna grow up to be nothin', but you made it! I love seeing that!" He gave me a pound plus a hug before mixing in with the gathering group near the Korean spot by the corner.

5:30 PM

I walked into the barbershop and headed straight to the back to see if my homie Mike was working. Mike is a master with the blade—responsible for some of the best cuts in the city, and the reason why most of the funny-looking guys in our neighborhood aren't single. Only he can make us ugly dudes look handsome. *I had a new essay coming out in a magazine*, I thought, *so why not celebrate it with a new fade?*

"Mike, how long?" I said, greeting everybody in the shop with "Hey, brother, how you been?"

"Come back tomorrow, D. Watk! And again, download the app and make an appointment, man, it's easy."

"Okay, okay, okay, man," I said, checking my phone and exiting the shop. My essay was thirty minutes away from dropping.

Mumbles, Fat Pat, and a group of other dudes were fussing by the store. I walked over to see what was up.

"Yo, I told y'all to close y'all shop at five. We gotta get money too!" a spindly dude in a North Face yelled at Fat Pat. His hand was by his waist, possibly ready to pull out a pistol. He didn't, but he looked ready. "Go ahead, roll out!" he said.

Fat Pat swung twice, barely connecting. The skinny dude dipped and gathered himself. Mumbles jumped in the middle, trying to break up the fight. He grabbed Fat Pat, saying, "Yo, chill, chill, hol' up!" The skinny dude threw a long punch, hitting Fat Pat and Mumbles, and that's when the brawl started. Two sets of dudes started beating on each other over drug sales.

People flock to fights as if free money is being given out. Everybody from the barbershop and the other side of the block rushed to see what was happening. The skinny dude reached back in his waistline, drew his pistol, and then popped a couple of rounds off. The bulk of us hit the deck. A few darted back into the barbershop. No one was hit.

I popped up and wiped the dirt off my pants.

"D. Watk, you good?" Mumbles said, brushing off his jacket.

"No, man, my phone screen cracked! Sike, man, I'm good." I laughed. "Let's get out of here. You wanna grab a drink?"

"Always!"

7:30 PM

Mumbles and I leaned on my Honda. The front fender was as broke as we were. Grip tape and luck held the car together. I sparked a cig, took a pull, and passed it.

"Man, y'all crazy," I said. "I'm too old to be ducking shots. I think I tore a ligament or something."

He laughed and said, "Boy, you silly, I know you joking but it's really no joke out here.

"Bro, I wanna get out. You feel me, bro? Crack game dead and it's different out there. Dry, broke, basically gone. That's why people get banged up every day. But these felonies, man, these felonies."

Mumbles's drug charges basically made him a partial citizen. Partial because they prohibited him from receiving student loans, public housing, and government assistance, and jobs that pay livable wages aren't breaking their necks to hire felons. So, what's a brother to do?

"Well, the first round on me," I said, taking one last puff of the cigarette. "But we drinking the cheap stuff!"

Mumbles patted me on the back as we walked inside. "Cheap liquor? Ain't professors rich, don't they got dat money?"

I laughed and replied, "I'll explain."

8:00 PM

My phone died. I didn't get to see my essay go live. I didn't care. Mumbles and I rapped four years of stories in three hours—laughing at the ups and downs, saluting the fallen, and being thankful for our lives. Drinking until our livers ached, but most importantly, we celebrated the love we have for being from Down Da Hill.

"Ain't nothing like being from Down Bottom! Down and dirty. We can get with anything and we still here, you feel me?" he said, holding his glass close to his face. "I'm trying to tell you, D. Watk, they ain't built like us, they couldn't walk an inch in our boots. You feel me, blood. I love you!

"Salute to all the real ones, all Eastside Baltimore all day, man!" he closed. It was familiar, what we'd always say, even back when we were nine or ten, fighting to make it off our blocks. We were still here, which was a blessing as our only currency was our own resiliency. I staggered in the front door at three in the morning and flopped on the couch with all of my clothes on. *Don't fall asleep*, I told myself, *without popping three Excedrins for the hangover that was coming, drinking a large cup of tap water, and charging your phone.*

I plugged in my cell and sunk into the couch. As I dozed, my phone came back on with a buzz, followed by another, and another. I thought the notifications were probably emails from some bill collectors who didn't understand that my financial situation hadn't changed since our conversation two days ago, so I turned it off.

Morning seems to always come when you get comfortable. The sun beamed through the curtains onto my face. I turned over and tried to cover my head with a pillow but the birds weren't having it; they had a lot to talk about that morning. I could hear cars driving past, construction, and everything else. I cut on my phone to check out my social media before I washed my face and brushed my teeth.

Thousands of Twitter notifications, emails, and Instagram followers were waiting. My poor phone could not handle the activity. It kept freezing as I tried to open the apps. I jumped up and grabbed my laptop, cracked it open, and started reading the emails—they were from news agencies wanting to connect with me and friends from college and high school telling me how I was this amazing writer. Apparently, I had fans, hundreds of new fans. How'd someone as broke as me get fans?

I shut the laptop. I had to take it all in for a second. "Too Poor for Pop Culture" had gone viral.

I dressed for work and headed to Coppin's campus—my phone going off nonstop. I was overwhelmed and still confused about what was happening. Before my story ran, Sarah had asked me to send in a picture of myself to accompany it, so I'd decided to get my homie David to take a photo of me at Old Town Mall since I spent so much time there. Before long, that image of me was all over Facebook, Twitter, and Instagram.

I caught the elevator up to the fourth floor in the building where the adjunct offices are located. A young-faced kid with dreads in slim jeans and big Nikes was getting on as I exited. "Wait a second," he said. "Are you *the* D. Watkins? The D. Watkins? Oh my God!"

He jumped off the elevator and gave me a suffocating hug. "Sir, I want to be just like you! I'm here looking for you! I read some of your *Salon* work!"

"Some of my *Salon* work?" I asked. "I only got one essay on the site."

"And it's the best essay I ever read. Please be my advisor!" he asked.

I wasn't even sure if adjuncts were allowed to advise. I mean, I needed advice for my own struggling career. I told the dude to follow me to the adjuncts' office so I could find out. As we walked down the hall, everybody broke their necks to congratulate me for emerging as the new voice of the people. Who knew writing one essay would give me the title of "voice of the people"? In my opinion, I definitely did not earn it. The whole thing seemed weird to me.

This kept happening as the day continued. People were treating me like a celebrity. It was all funny to me because I still didn't have enough money to make it to the end of the week. A few local radio stations and live internet streaming shows reached out, wanting me to come on to talk about the essay. There were messages from all of the Baltimore changemakers, politicians, and major television executives like David Simon, who created *The Wire*. I even autographed a white dude's arm at a deli. My essay was everywhere—and *Salon* reached out to let me know that I could definitely publish with them again.

I was in the game.

I did some radio spots that day and attempted to create a schedule before heading down to Old Town Mall to get a haircut. Mumbles and everybody else were out front.

"Bro, I had a hangover this morning, you feel me?" Mumbles admitted. "Like, I'm never drinking again till later on!"

I sat out front and cracked jokes long enough to burn a Newport and a Black & Mild. Everybody from my neighborhood is funny. We got Chris Rocks, Tiffany Haddishes, and Dave Chappelles all over the place.

"Yo, y'all crazy. I'm going to see Mike!" I said, walking into the barbershop.

It was packed, as usual, breathing room only. I made my way to the back, greeting everyone in the same way I always do. I always make it a point to greet everyone, my grandma didn't play with that. You walk in a room, you say "hello." It's that simple.

"Mike, how long?" I asked.

"You make an appointment?"

"Nah, man, they was shootin' outside and my essay came out! I forgot!"

"No appointment, no haircut. See you tomorrow, D. Watk!"

I left the shop defeated, feeling as if I would never get a haircut and be stuck with this little Florida Evans bush forever. What's funny is that this was the first part of my day where no one mentioned my essay. As I've mentioned before, access to information is class based.

I sat in my car and cracked the window. More emails and requests were popping up. Most sounded the same, all except one from a local reporter.

My name is ****** ******, and I am a reporter at *City Paper*. I read your piece "Too Poor for Pop Culture" in *Salon*, and I have to say it was quite compelling.

He went on to say, "There were also some comments underneath that caught my eye alleging you misrepresented your personal situation," and that he checked my Instagram and saw pictures of me on trips, hanging in nice hotel rooms, and pictures of a Rolex watch.

After that he asked a stupid question and quoted a piece of my essay as if he had cracked a case. "I wanted to ask if you could comment on how the pictures of luxury items and fancy trips square with this description of yourself: 'I have a little more than my friends but still feel their pain. My equation for survival is teaching at two colleges, substituting, freelance Web designing, freelance graphic designing, rap video director, wedding photographer and tutor—the proceeds from all of these are swallowed by my mortgage, cigarettes, rail vodka and Ramen noodles. I used to eat only free-range organic s●●●, I used to live in Whole Foods, I used to drink top shelf—I used to be able to afford pop culture.'

"The oldest of these pictures is five months ago," he wrote.

He finished by saying that he was giving me a chance to explain myself as if he was the authority on my life or knew anything about the black experience. I didn't know any better at the time, so I replied to his email, explaining how broke I was. The watch was a gift from a dead friend and other people took me to events in Africa and Europe on their dime because they believed in a potential that I didn't even know I had, or they just wanted to hang around me. And yes, I had an agent, but that doesn't translate into money.

We spoke on the phone briefly. I didn't like his tone and couldn't understand why he was trying to ruin me. I asked if he'd meet me near Old Town Mall so that I could give him a clear picture of who I was and where I'm from. He declined, saying he had enough for his story.

This is one of the biggest problems with journalism today. A person with an opinion on black culture who probably doesn't know any real black people still has the luxury to comment on and write about black life. I could've easily walked him through my block, introduced him to people, and expanded his perspective, but his mind was already made up. You'd think he'd know that Instagram is not really instant. Instead of using our exchange to congratulate me on the success of my article, or give me some pointers on journalism, he just tried to tear me down.

To make matters worse, the source this journalist based his story on was an Uncle Tom type I had one class with at the University of Baltimore, where I completed my undergrad, years before I published the essay. The kid was black but seemed like he had a fetish for sucking up to all things white and I know it did not take him long to develop a reputation for being a liar based on what I heard about him—because I didn't know him personally or anything about his life, as he didn't know anything about mine.

But other students from the writing program, who knew him better than I did, would make fun of him for saying that he was winning fellowships that didn't exist, writing for TV shows that forgot to put his name in the credits, and how going deep-sea diving for snow crabs in Alaska changed his life. In the comment section of my essay, this clown said that Douglass Homes in East Baltimore wasn't a housing project, but a nice senior citizen complex. Douglass Homes is a housing project, and everyone from Baltimore or who writes about Baltimore should know that. The reporter could have simply Googled or fact-checked his source to know that he should not have been taken seriously.

No matter the source, I was the guy with the newfound success, so the burden of proof was on me. The reporter dropped his article and my agent said that some major publishing companies wanted to sign me, but they had questions about what they'd read in the *City Paper* article. I guess the reporter and some of those editors thought a black guy from the streets like me can't be complex or funny or nuanced. This kind of thinking is easy to believe if you don't know anyone like me or frequent black neighborhoods like mine.

I remember pulling up by the alley with my face all twisted and heading toward the barbershop on the day that the reporter's story dropped.

"D. Watk. What's wrong, D. Watk?" Mumbles asked.

"So, my essay blew up, dug! Like I'm the man in the essay world right now, or at least I think so, and this coon, this corny lil Uncle Tom I went to school with, is telling lies and saying I'm rich."

"Damn, you ain't even got your own cigs, you feel me!" Mumbles laughed, handing me a Newport. I took it and sparked it.

"All I know is that when I see him, I'm busting his head wide open and probably the reporter too!"

"Reporter too? Is the reporter a white boy?" Mumbles asked.

I nodded yes.

"Yo, chill on the white reporter. He a white professional. Let him breathe. You'll get life for touchin' him. But we gonna get that other dude."

"Bet!"

✳

I held my own little investigation. It didn't take long for some former students who attended undergrad with us and a few professors who were proud of my new success to point me in his direction, as they were all equally mad at the Uncle Tom's actions.

The culprit hung out at basement readings, campus bars, and little hipster art functions. They told me who his crush was, gave me his phone number, and let me in on some of the other cruddy things that he had done. Perhaps they thought that I was going to confront him and talk it out peacefully like an after-school special or something. They had it wrong—I've slapped the teeth out of people's mouths for far less.

All day I envisioned myself splitting his head in half like a sunflower seed, cracking the seed open and crunching the shell with the heel of my boot, repeatedly. His pain clouded my thoughts when I woke up, while I brushed my teeth, after breakfast, on my way to Coppin and then Sojourner. I pulled up and parked next to my good friend Darnell Baylor, who was a student at the time. He was getting out of his car.

Baylor is a soul brother—a laid-back type, always fly with or without designer, and can rock the shell-toe Adidas and Air Jordans or the Birkenstocks with the kente cloth or a hoodie or mix and match both. He was a star running back at Dunbar, where we attended high school, and knows the streets and uses all of that knowledge to help juvenile offenders stay out of trouble. Baylor has always been a great friend, which is why I was triple excited when I found out he was taking my English class.

"Bro, I see your essay did numbers! It's on now, you about be everywhere!" he said. "You're gonna have a *New York Times* bestseller next. Watch what I tell you!"

"Man, I don't gotta book deal, and I might not get one now."

"What?"

Then I told him about the reporter, showed him the story, and explained the whole ordeal.

"Brother, listen. They can't stop you from shining," Baylor said. "You from these streets. You know these blocks and projects like the back of your hand, and you can write. Boy, you out here for us! They ain't us, man, forget them. They'll fade away and you'll be here, brother. Look what you been through! They can't stop you!"

Baylor started telling me that he shared the essay with some of the kids he counsels, and how they took a liking to my work. "You know how powerful that is? People who don't really read, really reading your work!"

"I'm honored and all that, bro," I said. "But those dudes gotta pay. They trying to end my career before it even start and I can't have that. I linked with Mumbles, we gonna bust their heads wide open."

Baylor walked off, shaking his head, and then came back, looking me dead in the eyes. "Are you crazy?! That's not your life. D. Watk is gone. You can't hit a person, man, you are a popular writer now. You don't see it but I do! These white people know you. The hood know you, but the white money know you now too. What Jay say?"

We both rapped, "Look, if I shoot you, I'm brainless. But if you shoot me, then you're famous."

What's a brother to do?

"I ain't no celeb though," I said. "And they really disrespected me."

"For one, touching that white reporter will probably get you the death penalty." Baylor laughed. "But all jokes aside, man, let it go. It ain't worth it. You'll see, bro, you are on your way."

I ended class early that day. I read the story a thousand times and it didn't seem as bad as I thought, but still, I couldn't stop thinking about what the reporter wrote and Baylor's words about how my life could really be different. If we were in the street, I'd have to do something, it wouldn't be a choice. As an adjunct professor and professionally unemployed freelancer, I couldn't just stomp out the journalist and his source, feel happy, and continue my day. Maybe D. Watk could get away with that, but not D. Watkins.

I needed to move in a different way because now I had a platform to highlight the issues that mattered to me.

I applied for a few writing jobs. Of course, no one hired me. I was still broke; however, all wasn't lost. *Salon, Aeon, The Guardian*, NPR, and a couple other media outlets reached out to me for some freelance work. I even got a call from the paper that ran that trash story on me. Publishing companies were taking notice, and I finally got that call from Barbara.

My phone buzzed while I was eating lunch with some of my

students at Friendship Academy, the charter school in East Baltimore where I occasionally worked as a substitute teacher.

"D., I've been waiting to make this call for two years," Barbara said. "Grand Central just made me an offer for *The Cook Up*!"

I blew up on the inside, muting Barbara and telling the kids that I got a book deal and I'm not going to have to sub at their filthy little school anymore because I'm about to get paid! And then I quickly humbled myself when I heard Barbara tell me how much the deal was worth. Still excited, I thanked her, got off the phone, and said, "Hey kids, I was joking. You know I love y'all and this school!"

One of the students replied, "Was the money funny, Watkins?" We all laughed.

"Nah, I'm new at this," I said. "I want y'all to remember that you can make money doing anything, if you are good at it."

I continued to publish articles throughout the rest of 2014, was invited out to some places to speak, and my friend Brandi from high school agreed to become my manager.

Then I was contacted by David Talbot, founder of *Salon*.

He emailed to say he was starting a new publishing company and Robert Kennedy Jr., Daniel Ellsberg, and Rebecca Solnit had all agreed to put out books with him. He then said he wanted to add me to the list:

I've been a big admirer of your writing in *Salon*, and I know that you're currently working on a memoir for another publisher. But if you're interested in hearing more about Hot Books, I'd love to kick around some possible ideas with you. Please let me know a good number and day/time to reach you.

Now, I was doing okay, but I didn't consider myself to be doing so well that I would be on a list with Robert F. Kennedy Jr. and Rebecca Solnit. I thought the dude was crazy. I gave him a call anyway.

"Hey man, it's D. Watkins. I'm responding to your email."

Excitedly he told me how much he loved my writing, referencing certain essays and telling me how *Salon* got daily bomb threats back when he ran it. I quickly learned how much he loved to buck the system. He said he'd love to put my essays in a book and offered me some money. I accepted it.

Now I was going into 2015 with two book deals. Baylor was right, people were paying attention and I had a bigger mission—suddenly, the reporter, his story, the dude that lied about me, and anything outside of that mission didn't matter because the biggest win for them is me putting myself in a position where I can't write, where I can't tell my story. And me not telling my story easily gives them the space to kill me, which wasn't happening—I'm not going anywhere.

6

NO RETIREMENT FOR
THE HUSTLERS

Why do we condemn people who are in and out of prison, but never address the system that prohibits ex-offenders from successfully reentering society?

I pulled over in front of my aunt's house so I could run in and take a whiz. Six pounds on the door before Fat Man yelled across the yard, "She not home, dummy. You just missed her!"

"Lemme use your bathroom, bro!"

He cracked the door as I ran past the small group of dudes hanging in front of the complex. They were playing cards, talking trash, and trading insults.

A steamy funk greeted me at the door, like a locker room for forty- to fiftysomethings. Clothes decorated the floor—I tried not to step on them but couldn't help planting my feet on a few. The bathroom was dirty. I aimed for the center of the brown-tinted water in the rusted bowl and flushed with the tip of my Nike. A white bar of soap with beige edges lay on the rim of the sink. I just used water.

I glanced in the kitchen on the way out. Fat Man, Mumbles's older brother, was taking empty gel caps out of a plastic bag and placing them into a drawer next to his fridge. Now I got the dirty soap, stink, and overall grimness—I was in a trap house.

A trap house is a place where illegal drugs are bought, sold, packaged, and stored. The word "trap" is pretty self-explanatory. Once you start, death or jail are the only two destinations, so we call it a trap.

"Yo, you want some water, bro?" Fat Man said, opening a twenty-four pack of Deer Park. "I got chips too!"

"Bring the water out front, homie," I replied. "I can't chill in a trap house, man, plus it stink in here."

He laughed and followed me out front with three waters and a bag of Rap Snacks, the flavor with a picture of Fabolous on the front. Fat Man tossed me a bottle of water and flopped down on a busted office chair. In front of him was a makeshift table constructed of a milk crate and half of a broken-off door. Teenage boys lined each corner of the complex. Their heads tilted toward their phones until customers walked up. Middle-aged black dudes, white men in Under Armour and work boots, and a slew of El Salvadorian guys dressed like construction workers. The game is the same as it has been: one kid collects the money and sends a signal to another kid who fetches the product and over and over again like clockwork.

"How ya brova doin'?" I asked.

"He prolly gonna beat that drug charge," Fat Man said, shaking his head. "But he washed on that 'temp murder."

I hadn't seen Mumbles since I disappeared to finish writing *The Beast Side* and hadn't really had time to hang with most of the dudes in front of the barbershop. "Yo, if he needs anything," I said, "tell him to hit my phone."

"Grandpa! We almost out," a thin but heavily tattooed woman with small square teeth yelled. "We almost done, you can come out in like thirty."

"Hurry up, Lil Man," Fat Man yelled at her. "I'm tryin' eat too! Damn!"

She looked him up and down, laughed, shook her head, squinted her eyes, and said, "You ain't ruinin' my Sunday, but shut ya mouth before I shut it for you." She gave me and another dude a handshake and walked over to stand next to the kid who was collecting the money.

"They not your workers?" I asked Fat Man. "This ya strip, right?"

"Nah, they work for her," he replied. "I can't sell a thing until the kids say it's okay. They got the muscle, the weapons, they out here."

Fat Man used to be a legend. Mumbles used to brag about him all day, starting every sentence with, "Yo, my big brova said . . ." Fat Man is God's height, wide as a row house, and stays covered in diamonds. He never ratted, isn't a hater, and always makes everyone laugh. He's a real OG who loves to spit out his grandmother's wisdom and hand twenties to all of the kids before they chased the ice-cream truck. I'm not sure how or why he got in the drug game, but I do know he ran it like a champ.

"Man, I was in jail too long, lil bro," Fat Man said, removing some bags of weed and gel caps from his pocket, placing them under the crate. "The team is gone, the block has changed, and I'm just out here tryin' to live."

✳

Fat Man sat in federal prison for about eight years for drug distribution. He came home, lived in a halfway house, and created a plan to stay out of prison, just like Mumbles was trying to do. His version consisted of working two or three jobs until he saved up enough money to buy a dump truck.

"Wit a dump truck," he explained, "I could get money in the blizzard. When it's hot out, all that. The one I want cost like twenty-eight to thirty thousand at the auction. I'm tryin' to stack. I filled out apps everywhere. Ain't no work out here for me."

My aunt pulled up with some grocery bags. I helped her carry them into the house. She put them away and joined me on the front steps, asking me about work. I responded, "Work is cool." I couldn't help but watch Fat Man in action. Well, it wasn't much action—he mostly lounged in the chair and waited, every once in a while a straggler would wander by and make a purchase. I saw about four sales over two hours. Fat Man was in pain; he looked like the before model in a Bengay ad. Dude was slow, too slow to outrun anything—and slanging dope is a young person's game. You should be sharp, agile, ripped, and able to dip, duck, hide, and fit into small places. A few people stopped to crack jokes and I saw him hesitantly passing money to a woman that only yelled at him, though he mostly sat alone.

"Big fella," I said, walking in his direction, "it's crazy out here, be careful." He got up to give me a handshake and a hug.

"All I can do. If you hear anything about a job, bro, holla at me. Mumbles told me you doin' okay out here wit da writin'," he said, giving me a half hug with a handshake. "Janitor, dog walker, rental cop, whatever. I'll do anything to get from up and around here, you hear me. I'm tryin' work. And I know it's not what you know, it's who you know, D. Watk. I know you!"

"I'll try," I told him as I walked back to my car. He thanked me too many times. I turned around to yell, "No problem." The sun fell on his wet eyes and sad smile. "Take care!" I said one more time before pulling off. There is no retirement for the hustlers.

I'm an artist, not a reentry expert, and have little to no experience getting companies to hire ex-offenders but I do care and want to help. I've put a good word in for a few of my friends who spent some time in jail and some were hired, only because of my connections. I should mention that they were not high-paying jobs, but they made enough to leave the streets alone—well, some did, anyway. The hard truth is that everyone does not have connections. Going to jail as a poor person is easy, going to jail as a poor black person is even easier, and so many people who are lucky enough to survive prison like Fat Man have nothing to come home to. Hustling until something falls into place, just like Mumbles will have to do if he ever makes it home, is the reality for many.

I really wish people knew that drug dealing isn't that glamorous. They should create a job where people like Fat Man and Mumbles tour schools, talking to kids about how non-lucrative the game really is and how the pay doesn't match the countless hours. Trap houses in Hollywood movies, on records, and in TV land are overexaggerated. Most aren't that great and the people in them aren't making millions of dollars. When a smug college professor appeared with me on an Al Jazeera TV show and foolishly said, "The problem is that kids in inner cities like Baltimore don't want factory jobs, they want to make hundreds of thousands of dollars a month selling drugs," I almost died laughing.

I asked him, "Who makes $100,000 off of crack nowadays? And where are the factory jobs in Baltimore? This isn't 1960!" This is just another example of a guy who gets to comment on a world that he doesn't live in, have a connection to, or understand.

Meanwhile, Fat Man is unemployed, wants a job, and probably has dudes like the professor's perspectives thrown in his face.

We have to be the generation that changes this. My friends and I are sick of seeing our loved ones go in and out of prison. The Ban the Box campaign was set up to advocate for removing any questions about prior criminal activity from job applications—giving ex-offenders a fair shot at gaining employment with livable wages. To date, their campaign has been successful in forty-five cities including Baltimore and in the states of Hawaii, California, Colorado, New Mexico, Minnesota, Massachusetts, and Connecticut. Their progress is amazing, but we still need more. Many of those states have online databases where anyone can gain civil or criminal background information as long as you can spell a person's name correctly.

Under the current system, many people like Fat Man will never get a job. He'll end up back in prison on the taxpayers' dime, dead, or in the street that he's too old to be hustling on, which will land him back in prison. In Baltimore, it's hard enough to stay out of jail as an innocent black man, and once you've been placed in the system, it's a wrap.

PART 2

THE BIGGEST GANG IN AMERICA

7

AN AMERICAN TRADITION

The one unified organization that's dedicated to separating the white and black elite from the poor, especially poor African Americans, is the cops—one time, 12, five-0, flatfoots, boys in blue, Jakes, fuzz, the law, or whatever you call them. Police officers are the official gatekeepers, the ones responsible for the past and current divides. The guys who often prohibit social mobility.

Cops in poor neighborhoods and cops in rich neighborhoods are two completely different types of guys—not Burger King and McDonald's different but night and day. The difference is simple: cops in rich neighborhoods protect and serve the rich, and cops in poor neighborhoods terrorize the poor.

I was sitting in the passenger seat of a car traveling down a street in an affluent Philadelphia neighborhood. Big houses, manicured lawns, luxury cars, and juice bars were all over the place. The driver was a black filmmaker—not a well-known one, but rich and from privilege nonetheless. I thought the dude was driving too fast for no reason, and I was right because sirens and flashing blue-and-red lights popped right out of the bushes.

His car was clean, no weed scent, and no open containers, so it seemed like we'd get away with a ticket.

"Oh God! What do they want?!" he screamed, beating on his steering wheel. "I really don't feel like this right now!"

I was checking my seat belt, cutting the music down, and leaning my chair up. I also dug in my bag, grabbed my glasses, and threw them on. The driver was boiling as if he wasn't wrong—dude's nostrils flared, every vein plump and pulsing as his heavy breathing fogged the windows.

"License and registration, please," said the buzz-cut cop. He had one of those New Jersey Turnpike faces, you know, the ones that hand out $300 fees and court visits.

"What did we do?!" the dude responded. "You picked the right black man to stop! I live here, I pay taxes! Just like my father! Here's my paperwork, bring your badge number back and an apology!"

I'm not sure what was more surprising, the dude getting mad at the cop for stopping him for speeding or seeing a cop use words like "please" and "thank you."

"I'm going to let you go," the cop said. "But you need to slow it down some, buddy, and be careful." He passed the paperwork back to the driver.

"I wasn't speeding! You're taking time out of my day for nothing! I still want your badge number!"

The officer passed us a card and said, "Have a good day."

Dude sped off like he had a point to prove. I was thankful that the situation hadn't turned ugly, because in poor neighborhoods it doesn't work like that.

First of all, cops don't say things like "please" and "have a good day"—it's against their job description; a speeding luxury car in my section of East Baltimore would've got a first-class trip to the pavement followed by an all-inclusive stay at Central Booking.

We are used to police brutality, we know it's illegal, but it is what it is. That mouthing off would've surely got his face smashed in around my way.

East Baltimore cops don't ask questions. They jump out with cocked guns and wave them at crowds of people. It doesn't really matter if you are guilty or not, that's a tax for being poor and you have to learn how to survive in those situations.

I drove flashy, I drove sport, I drove cheap—and I always operate the same way. Driving while black is like always traveling with a thousand bricks of cocaine in your trunk. It doesn't matter if you work as an accountant or a camp counselor, you have to drive like a drug lord, which means he or she must play the music just barely loud enough to hear, know and follow all of the speed limits, sit straight up, keep both hands on the steering wheel, and universally agree with everything that the police officer says. Even after he gives you a ticket for going 46 in a 45, you have to agree.

No one is scared of police officers, we all know that most of them are cowards—that's why they reach for their guns so quick—but what's the alternative? Disagreeing with a police officer can get you a bigger ticket, thrown in prison, or a head shot. Who wants to risk that?

Cops in poor neighborhoods are extremely petty and fueled by pointless stats like clearance rates that never lead to real convictions. Most are completely disconnected from the communities they serve. Well, some are disconnected, and others are both disconnected and brutal.

The Department of Justice has investigated Cleveland, Baltimore, and Ferguson within the past few years and has found hundreds of cases of officers breaking the law, being racist, excessively harassing African Americans, selling drugs, using drugs on the clock, and a bunch of other incidents that would make you think every city and state would be tougher on police, but that doesn't matter. Nothing changes—we are forced to deal with this racist system.

The marching, the protests, the riots, and the hiring of minority cops have all failed. Racist police officers are an American tradition—it's as American as high-fructose corn syrup.

OUR COPS

Qualifications for becoming a Baltimore City police officer:

- Age of at least twenty years and nine months at the time of application
- US citizen
- Have a high school diploma or GED
- Have a valid driver's license
- Have no felony convictions
- Meet prior-drug-use standards

Becoming a cop doesn't instantly make you a hero. It means you met the basic qualifications as listed above, finished academy, and were granted a badge and a gun. We must stop calling all cops "heroes" as it is as dangerous as any other unfair stereotype assigned to any group of people. It's also the reason why killer cops who murder unarmed African Americans are rarely charged and usually get to keep their jobs.

Back in 2015, State's Attorney Marilyn Mosby brought charges against the officers involved in Freddie Gray's killing at a time when holding crooked cops accountable for their crimes might as well have been illegal itself. You'd think that the so-called good cops would champion her determination, right? Why would they support officers who stopped a guy for no reason and caused his death? But, of course, they remained silent on the matter or loudly supported their fellow officers. In the end, none of the cops involved in Freddie Gray's death were convicted of any charges. Some would argue against the tactics prosecutors used, blaming them for allowing the officers to walk; however, I don't think any prosecution tactic could have defeated the all-cops-are-heroes narrative. Gray was branded as the bad black guy and his arresting officers were the heroes who fight for justice.

Countless TV shows, Bruce Willis movies, and novels push stories of honorable police officers who use their badges only in the service of good. Many of us who have not had positive experiences with the law just can't relate. African Americans and other oppressed groups have been complaining about cops for years, even before Gray's killing, but we were ignored or written off as crazy.

We are not crazy.

Take a walk through any poverty-stricken neighborhood and ask a resident to tell you a few stories about police officers. Their bad experiences will always outweigh the good. And many of the black officers who hail from those neighborhoods don't make a difference in their racist departments as they're breaking their backs to assimilate to the established culture of law enforcement. They do little or nothing to create change in the system, allowing the cycle to continue. Police officers do whatever they want and we have no recourse, because who listens to poor black people?

Cops know this; that's why it's so easy for them to act reckless. After Gray's killing and the implementation of consent decrees, which federally documented the problems in policing and offered solutions, you'd think cops would tighten up. However, cops don't make any changes in their behavior because they are rarely held accountable.

In 2017, while Baltimore was supposed to be going through police reform, a group of officers led by Officer Richard A. Pinheiro Jr. were caught on body-cam footage planting evidence on an innocent black kid who they arrested but would have had to release. Pinheiro has since been charged and found guilty, but only after the video went viral. You think he would've been charged if the judge had to rely solely on the word of the black kid he'd set up? Of course not, because "all cops are heroes" and they wouldn't do something as bad as planting evidence, right? It's important to mention that all of Pinheiro's time was suspended. He was lucky enough to walk away with community service, without spending any time behind bars—meaning that the kid he planted drugs on did more jail time than Pinheiro, the actual criminal.

Justice?

GTTF TALES: NOTORIOUS P.I.G.S.

You ever heard of the Gun Trace Task Force (GTTF)? Think of the crooked cop Denzel Washington played in *Training Day*. Now multiply that by eight. The all-cops-are-heroes myth is the reason why the GTTF case has been grossly underreported, despite its lurid details. Revealing to America the convictions and plea deals from this collection of crooked cops should change that hero-cop narrative permanently, but I doubt it will because even the GTTF are being written off as a few bad apples.

Many residents of Baltimore know these clowns, especially homies like me who were raised in the culture of police brutality. Although outsiders were surprised to learn about the city's elite GTTF—eight cops, including Evodio Hendrix, Maurice Ward, Daniel Hersl, Marcus Taylor, Jemell Rayam, and Momodu Gondo, led by Sergeant Wayne Jenkins and Thomas Allers— who were granted special outside-the-box privileges in an effort to get firearms off the streets. With those special privileges they created one of the most notorious gangs in the history of Baltimore, using the protection of their badges to do everything from extort working citizens and drug dealers to selling drugs, instigating murders, destroying families, and draining the already struggling city's budget with overtime fraud.

The city's problem with guns and violent crime is no secret: Baltimore has recorded more than a thousand murders over the last three years, and its crime rate is ten times the national average. *The City Paper* found that New York, with a population fourteen times larger, has had only 977 murders in the same time frame.

Every national media outlet ran to Baltimore when a few cars were torched and a couple of buildings got tossed in protest after Freddie Gray was killed, but these dirty-cop cases received a fraction of the coverage.

Our country does an amazing job of hiding the truth about dirty cops, and a better job at keeping them out of prison. However, the system kind of worked this time as all eight of the officers involved in the task force have now been convicted on various charges.

GTTF OFFICER	SENTENCE
Daniel Hersl	18 years
Marcus Taylor	18 years
Wayne Jenkins	25 years
Thomas Allers	15 years
Jemell Rayam	(not sentenced yet; still snitching)
Momodu Gondo	(not sentenced yet; still snitching)
Maurice Ward	7 years
Evodio Hendrix	7 years

Let me take it back to the beginning. Back to when I watched my late brother, friends, and their workers separate money into multiple piles. They sold crack, heroin, and cocaine, exactly in that order. I rarely saw their drugs but I always—always—saw the money.

From what I remember, the first pile was for the crew leaders—they were stashing that. The second pile went to the lieutenants and underbosses, who'd take their cut out and use the rest to pay the workers. Pile three was for product re-up, supplies, and everything else you need to run a dope shop. And pile four got stuffed into a manila envelope and wrapped tight with rubber bands. They always joked around, calling that envelope the "taxes." Of course, they weren't actually paying taxes on their income or sales to the government, and they weren't setting aside contributions to a retirement plan. Their taxes went straight to the cops.

Yes, cops take money from drug dealers. Cops rape. Cops lie in their reports. Cops beat people. Cops sell drugs. Cops threaten citizens. Cops intimidate other cops. Cops are gang-affiliated. They'll snatch a blunt out of your hand and smoke it, hide extra guns in the dope house, aim their pistol at you for fun, plant drugs on you, make you sell drugs for them or with them, make you rob and steal, and then expect to be called a hero no matter what they've done. Still, most politicians—from those as progressive as Obama to those as racist as Trump—break their necks to cosign their hero status.

Earning a badge after applying for a job and completing a couple of months of training doesn't automatically make you a hero. Detective Sean Suiter, former GTTF member, was set to testify on the horrific crimes his coworkers committed; however, he was shot the day before his trial. The media have been passing it off as a suicide, even though Suiter had immunity and the evidence makes it look like a murder. Either way, he didn't make it to court.

The Baltimore Sun reported on the testimony of Detective Maurice Ward, who pleaded guilty to racketeering charges:

> The video opens with a group of Baltimore police officers prying open a safe, revealing thick stacks of cash held together by two rubber bands each.
>
> They call to their sergeant, Wayne Jenkins, who instructs the group not to touch anything and to keep the camera rolling—he wanted this one done by the book.
>
> Except, Detective Maurice Ward testified Tuesday, the officers already had pocketed half the $200,000 they found inside the safe before the recording started, after taking a man's keys during a traffic stop and entering his home without a warrant. It was one of many illegal tactics Ward said the officers used as they chased guns and drugs across the city while skimming proceeds for themselves.

Critics of the police department, street dudes, and annoyed people from the blocks I grew up on have been screaming this for years. We have been trying to call attention to corruption *for years*. But no one listened.

According to Ward, officers kept BB guns with them "in case we accidentally hit somebody or got into a shootout, so we could plant them." The officers tampered with criminal cases, even lying to the wife of a man they had locked up and stolen from, accusing him of infidelity so she would cut off her support. They went as far as writing her a letter, pretending to be a pregnant side chick. These clowns proudly profiled African Americans and stole as if it was part of their job description. And yet they still saw themselves as heroes. Abuse of power is an understatement here.

As I followed the GTTF case, listening to opinions and collecting information, one common narrative I heard was this: "Those cops only targeted criminals. They had to use special tactics to keep up with the everyday evolving world of crime, and everyday citizens weren't affected by their actions." This claim is problematic for a number of reasons. Let's use the case of a woman we'll call Jane Jones as an example.

Jones, a successful hair stylist in Baltimore, was targeted by the GTTF back in 2016. Her nice car caught the attention of Sergeant Wayne Jenkins, and he started watching her apartment, excitedly reporting suspicious activity to Officer Momodu Gondo. Jenkins then crafted a plan to raid her home for cash and other goods. He told Gondo that only they and Officer Daniel Hersl would be involved in this mission, no need to share the sting with other cops on the task force. He thought there would be $40,000 to $50,000 inside that the three could split. Hersl responded, "I can use the money, I'm in the process of buying a house."

The officers were caught on tape entering her complex.

Initially they were denied access by security until Hersl came in with a piece of paper and some police gear. The trio found no cash. However, they did retrieve 390 grams of heroin, gel caps, a digital scale, and a Chanel bag worth about $5,000. They turned in the drugs, along with the rest of the paraphernalia, and Gondo kept the purse and gifted it to a woman he was dating. Reporting the drugs wasn't an example of good police work—I believe it was a petty attempt to make Jones pay for not having cash in the house for the police officers to steal.

The counterargument rests on the 390 grams of heroin that came off of the street as a result of the officers' break-in. But that neglects the fact that the officers were not looking for drugs. Finding heroin was not part of their agenda. On a federal wiretap, Jenkins clearly stated they were looking for cash, and they just stumbled across the heroin by mistake—while using their badges as shields. There's also the question of where the drugs actually came from. They could have been planted in Jones's home, as the racketeering investigation proved members of the task force had done to frame others.

Finding drugs was never a part of their mission. That means that they were bad guys too. Actually, the GTTF are worse than the bad guys, because they stole after pledging to protect and serve the people of Baltimore. Meanwhile, our taxes paid their ridiculously high salaries and their fraudulent overtime.

Real police reform will never happen as long as we continue to make excuses for police officers when they break laws while celebrating every time they accomplish something they get paid to do. Our low standards are evident when we applaud cops reporting a drug bust, even after we find out their true intention was to steal.

✳

HOW GTTF'S DANIEL HERSL STALLED ONE RAPPER'S CAREER

After three decades in America, I witnessed justice for the first time. A jury found Daniel Hersl guilty of racketeering, robbery, and overtime fraud.

"Danny Hersl wasn't a part of this monster group. He wanted out. He wanted out right away," Steve Hersl, Daniel's brother, said outside of the courthouse after the verdicts were returned. "He was getting out two weeks before he got busted."

"He's devastated," Hersl's lawyer, William Purpura, added. "He has absolutely no criminal record. . . . He's been in jail now for close to eleven months and he, quite frankly, was hoping he would be coming home."

Hersl's brother and lawyer were funnier than a Chris Rock stand-up special. They were really acting as though he should be home. However, I understand where Hersl's brother and lawyer were coming from. They're on his side and are fortunate enough to have a platform to provide that support, thanks to news outlets willing to listen to their side of the story. Hersl's brother probably loves him dearly, and maybe he can't see him in the same light as the prosecutors and jury. We can.

This is how Hersl has affected our community:

Back in 2014, Kevron Evans, who raps under the name Young Moose, sat in a jail cell while his mixtape *Out the Mood 2* went viral, racking up millions of hits and downloads from mixtape sites and YouTube. Evans is from my neighborhood, so I was kind of aware of his work, but I didn't know how popular he really was until the kids at Friendship Academy, where I taught, put me down.

They only listened to Young Moose, and spent hours analyzing his lyrics and showing me his videos. They were excited to support a rapper who was doing well and telling stories about our neighborhood.

Next, I learned that Daniel Hersl was his arresting officer. At the time, I knew Hersl had been harassing people from our neighborhood for years—he'd been stealing money and beating people ever since he was a plainclothes cop. My friend Tip, who has been around longer than I have, reminded me of how well we knew Hersl, beyond the headlines.

"He's that cop that would walk by the carry-out on Broadway and slap the food out of people's hands!" Tip said, pacing back and forth. "Didn't matter if you mouthed off or not, he thought that stuff was funny. You remember that clown?" I did remember that clown, so I decided to report Young Moose's story for Baltimore's *City Paper*.

I did some research and found an article that reported the city had paid out nearly $200,000 in misconduct settlements between 2007 and 2014 in response to suits filed over Hersl's misconduct on the job. (I'm not sure where Hersl's brother was when the officer illegally harassed people, beat citizens, and cost the city money; leaving us taxpayers responsible for footing the bill.) I ended up writing about how Moose stimulates the local arts community through his music and how the settlements paid out in response to complaints about his arresting officer's behavior amounted to theft from city residents.

This is what Young Moose told me about Hersl, from a jail call: "He's a dirty cop and he has a personal vendetta against me.

He always lies on me and I only pleaded guilty to my last charge because he locked up a friend who wasn't supposed to go to jail. I can't remember a time when I wasn't bein' harassed by him. He even attacked my mother. She asked Hersl for a warrant during the raid and he said, 'You must be Moose's mother, I have something better!' and then locked her up."

Young Moose's arrest was heavily reported at the time, and he was portrayed as a bad guy who got what he deserved. But Moose stuck with his story and maintained his innocence. Now, the truth about Hersl has finally emerged. The sad part is that Moose had to sit in prison for over a year. Our city, our country, is full of so many similar stories, because dirty cops like Hersl are not often brought to justice.

The GTTF's criminal actions are not shocking to me because of what and who I know. Nevertheless, if this is what justice feels like, Hersl behind bars, I could get used to it.

8

HOW OUR TRUST IS UNDONE

The justice never lasts.

If you are poor and black in America, you live in a police state.

It's been like that since before I was born, and I don't see any changes coming in the foreseeable future. I've acknowledged this system for a long time. It's one of the reasons I'm still alive. It's one of the reasons I'm rarely surprised by rogue police actions.

But every once in a while, even I get shocked: watching Eric Garner scream "I can't breathe!" on camera while on the receiving end of an illegal choke hold; seeing Officer Michael Slager shoot Walter Scott in the back for no reason; reading about the amount of time the Ferguson Police Department left Michael Brown, a teenager who was headed to college, on the ground after he was shot in the head by Officer Darren Wilson.

Now, we have Georgia.

A police cruiser dashcam captured officer Lieutenant Greg Abbott of Cobb County, Georgia, talking to a white suspect during a fairly routine DUI traffic stop. On the video, Abbott can be heard instructing the woman in the passenger seat to put her hands down. She responds in fear, "I've just seen way too many videos of cops . . ."

"But you're not black," Abbott interrupts. "Remember, we only kill black people. Yeah, we only kill black people, right? All the videos you've seen, have you seen white people get killed?"

I wish this was a joke. It's not.

It's bad enough that so many black families are suffering through tragedies created by police officers who are almost never held accountable for their actions. But how evil do you have to be to joke or brag about it? In this moment, Abbott shows no regard for human life . . . well, *black* human life.

According to Abbott's attorney, Lance LoRusso, his actions were nothing more than plain ole good policing. "Abbott's comments must be observed in their totality to understand their context," LoRusso said in a statement to the *Washington Post*. "He was attempting to de-escalate a situation involving an uncooperative passenger. In context, his comments were clearly aimed at attempting to gain compliance by using the passenger's own statements and reasoning to avoid making an arrest."

If this joke of a statement by LoRusso is true, then how would Abbott de-escalate a similar incident with a black person? Oh yeah: shoot them.

A collection of phony apologies from Abbott and the department followed LoRusso's statement. I'm sure that Abbot's sorry wasn't for saying what he said, but that we heard it. Despite the fact that police officers *should* be the main advocates for Abbott's termination, cops in general didn't call for his resignation.

My hope here is that the all-cops-aren't-bad people are paying attention. It's because of all-too-common interactions like this that we just don't trust police.

CHECK THEIR SYSTEM NEXT TO OURS

I got a call the other day from a homie who is currently serving time in federal prison. He's thirteen years in on a twenty-seven-year bid, to be exact. No weapons, no shoot-outs, no dangling people out of a window; he didn't live like Scarface. His time stems from nonviolent drug charges.

"Yo! D. Watk," he said. "Thanks for the pictures, bro! How you holding up?"

"I'm cool, brother, maintaining, out here trippin' off of this Trump guy."

"Yo, what he do now?" he replied.

It's funny how our incarcerated family wakes up to the same questions about this Trump guy as those of us on the outside. *What did he do now? Is America gone yet? Are we still a country?*

"So, check this out," I said. "Let's say Trump ran a dope strip, right. He's the boss and a bunch of his key underbosses and workers already got indicted, copped out, or admitted their wrongdoing to the feds. Man, his old campaign chairman Paul Manafort and deputy Richard Gates are fighting accusations of money laundering and tax fraud, and his former national security advisor Michael Flynn and campaign foreign policy advisor George Papadopoulos have both pleaded guilty to lying to the Feds!"

"Oh, the Feds don't play," he laughed. "So basically, what you saying is Trump about to go down this week? He coming inside here with me? Oh bro, I'ma steal his wig."

"No!" I laughed. "That's the crazy part!"

See, when my friend was arrested for those drug crimes, he and the other people wrapped up in the indictment were snatched up within the same few days. Federal agents didn't dance around mountains of evidence—they found no piles of drugs and stacks of guns, because they didn't exist. Still, they kicked in his door at 4 AM, slammed him on the floor, stomped him out in their work boots, told his crying daughter to "shut the f*ck up," and took him to the station. There he sat until they basically forced him to take the twenty-seven years. The prosecutor told him, "Take this twenty-seven or I'm pushing for sixty years, and our conviction rate is over 95 percent." So yeah, he had to take the time. We've been trying to keep his spirits up ever since.

A black man with drug charges gets a beating before being dragged into custody, while Trump, a person who might have worked with Russia to steal our highest office, gets to negotiate how he chooses to be interviewed by the special prosecutor after the people on his team lied? When did the Feds become so user-friendly? I understand that the president gets a certain amount of courtesy and I don't expect them to kick the White House door in or anything, but this is just getting silly.

"So, get this, bro," I said. "Mueller, the guy running the investigation, wants to interview Trump, but Trump's lawyers want him to get a set of written questions that he can complete on his own and send back in."

"Like a take-home test?"

"Like a take-home test!" I laughed. He laughed even louder. "Knowing Trump won't be the one answering those questions. He probably won't even see them! His lawyers said they don't want him to be interrogated by federal prosecutors because they fear that he might incriminate himself. I can't make this up."

"Ay, yoooo, ain't that the point? The Feds press people until they pop, right? They made some of the toughest gangstas in the world squeal," he said. "Man, I swear, it must feel good to be rich and white."

And that's the other America—the one people like my friend and I will never have access to. Knowing the special rights a person like Trump enjoys makes it easy to have no hope or trust in our system at all.

9

THE BALTIMORE UPRISING

Imagine a Sunday so beautiful that you decide to go out for a jog. Then suddenly you are stopped by a couple of police officers for no reason other than the color of your skin. You are beaten. Arrested without a charge. You are thrown in the back of a van after clearly stating that you need help for the pain that was just inflicted upon you. Your pleas are ignored.

The back of the van is dark. It has safety belts so that you won't tumble around during the ride. But instead of following protocol and locking you in, the officers decide to ignore your safety. As the van takes off you can feel every hard bump and curve of your city's unevenly paved streets. The officers make stop after stop while continuing to ignore your cries for medical attention.

You've already lost hope, and know that the officers won't do anything to help you. Your breath is gone and soon your consciousness will be too. They find you this way when they finally open the door. They have to get you to a hospital now. By the time the cops arrive at the nearest hospital it is too late. There's been too much damage done. You fight, but you die.

A concerned citizen caught the events leading up to your killing on a camera phone. It quickly went viral after it was posted on social media and then completely exploded after the world finds out that you are dead. Enraged, the people take to the streets in your name, burning police cars, smashing windows, and damaging a couple of storefronts—bucking the oppressive system that has had its foot on your neck for years. In an attempt to quell the people, the cops who are responsible for your death are charged.

It's a surprise that the cops are charged—only to be investigated by their own police department, which is not a surprise, and set free one by one with zero convictions. Not a single person is held accountable for the death of another unarmed black boy, our Freddie Gray.

FREDDIE DIED

"Everybody watches movies, D.! TV and movies!" my friend Rello said, dribbling a basketball against the pavement and in between his legs. "You gotta make a film. Not everybody gonna read books! But everybody watch the tube!" Some of our crew nodded in agreement. About twenty of us twenty- or thirtysomethings eclipsed the corner of Lakewood Street and Madison on a semi-warm April day. I was trying to get half of us down to Bocek Park for a five-on-five. "They reading my book, homie," I said. "I can sell!"

Everyone laughed and we traded a few more jokes as we limped our way down to the court. Limped because East Baltimore is rough on the bones—a lot of us have been beaten, shot, or suffered from some type of dirt bike injury.

Rello elevator-pitched me all the way from Lakewood down to the court. He had some great ideas, but I had to school him on how the pen is the foundation. "We can make a bunch of films or TV shows," I told him. "But somebody is writing them! Most of your favorite films were probably books first!"

We reached the park. Just like us, the court was also broken and beaten. The previous summer it was painted over with a fresh coat of red and blue. But the following Baltimore winter made sure its makeover was temporary. We didn't care; we just wanted to compete while knocking off a few pounds for the summer.

Three or four games in, a black Honda pulled up. Q., another guy from our block who used to ball with us, hopped out, squeezing his iPhone. I haven't seen him in person since he discovered Twitter.

"Yooooooo!!!!!" he said. "They killed that boy Freddie Gray from over west! Slim died today! Punk racist cops!"

Obvious rage exploded from our side of the gate as some crowded his phone and some reached for their phones to watch the video over and over again.

I didn't know Gray personally, but he was tight with my friend GD—black Baltimore is small like that, everybody knows everybody. GD always called him Peppa or Freddie Black because of his complexion. Gray was dark, slim in stature, stood 5' 7" or 5' 8", and had a reputation for being a friendly jokester. Everybody knew he liked to clown, which made the actions by the cops seem more evil.

Shortly after the news pronounced Freddie dead we took to the streets—some peaceful, some violent, but all in pain. We marched, screaming, "Justice for Freddie Gray!" Cop cars were flipped like stained mattresses, fights broke out, and a few buildings burned. It got so wild that the National Guard parked troops with heavy automatic weapons and Army trucks on residential blocks. Mayor Stephanie Rawlings-Blake issued a 10 PM curfew in the midst of the madness. I didn't have a press pass, but I'd scraped up enough clout as a freelance journalist to bypass the curfew law. I tagged along with some reporters from the *Sun, City Paper,* and *Guardian.* Together we documented the cocktail of pain and positivity that would grow to become the Baltimore Uprising.

Prior to the killing of Freddie Gray and the Baltimore Uprising, I had documented Black culture for a number of publications. I'd become a sort of go-to guy for a range of topics, including police brutality, literacy, the digital divide, and systemic racism.

With Gray's death, the major cable news networks became interested in my work. I could talk about the issues before a large audience with the hope that my words would have a greater impact. My TV experience at the time was limited. I had nothing under my belt except a few local news shows and HuffPost Live interviews. That was more than enough for the influx of reporters and producers that flooded every inch of Baltimore. The media were everywhere: Don Lemon at City Hall, Geraldo Rivera on the corner of Penn and North, Anderson Cooper mobbed by fans, and on and on and on. They were snagging everybody who was anybody to do interviews on Gray, our cop problem, and the current state of the city.

"Okay D., three shows reached out, they want to talk about your *New York Times* piece," said Brandi, my manager. "I'll send you the location and hit times." The previous day, I had penned an essay for the *Times* titled "In Baltimore, We're All Freddie Gray" on our city's ugly history of police brutality and how growing up black in Baltimore under Mayor Martin O'Malley almost guaranteed constant harassment and an arrest record.

The first few TV interviews went smooth. I talked about the collection of peaceful protests that went down, and how I and other community members were going to play our part in repairing the damage. I also got a chance to shed light on the many systemic issues that cause all of these cop shootings. I might not have been the most effective communicator, but at least I was able to get my main points across. I felt confident about all of my media appearances that afternoon and got a chance to show that every black person isn't the same. I planned on pushing the same message that night on CNN and was looking forward to being on *OutFront* with Erin Burnett.

CNN was posted up on the corner near the park in front of City Hall. I strolled up to the set, prepared to give the same spiel. Erin introduced the guests—me and some square ex-cop named Dan Bongino, who was over at CNN studios in Washington or New York or somewhere. I started by talking about the positive things that were going on in the city and even slipped in some jokes about how the peace rallies were so diverse that they looked like a Black Eyed Peas concert or a Gap commercial.

"D.'s words are inflammatory and irresponsible!" screeched a voice in my right ear. "It is horribly irresponsible for him to even mention 'burn to the ground' in an op-ed piece because he's going to be the first one running away when the fire starts!" It was Bongino. They had told me he was a Republican who would position himself against me, but who knew the little guy would come out swinging like that?

"I mention 'burn to the ground,' but no, I'm not running anywhere!" I replied.

"Yeah, you are running."

"No, I'm not running anywhere. I'm right here. I'm not going anywhere. I mentioned 'burn to the ground' in the op-ed piece because the city was burning, that's what was happening."

Bongino kept slipping in little jabs so I started talking over him, "You read it but you probably couldn't comprehend it, you don't know what it's like growing up black in a city like Baltimore. You don't know what it's like to be harassed and brutalized every day! You have a police background so you are protecting your fellow gang members, so I understand where you are coming from!"

His early claims were naive and disconnected—I've never run from anything in my life, not even the police, well, maybe the police. I kept cutting him off, feeling that his foolish statements gave me no choice. The smell of the streets still reeks from my pores, so yeah, I lost it. I felt like I was perpetuating the angry-black-man stereotype that the mainstream media love to portray.

I was upset with my performance. Dismayed that a fake talking head could make me snap like that. If we were on set together, I probably would've punched him in the face. But I couldn't punch him in the face because I'm not D. Watk anymore. I'm D. Watkins.

Surprisingly, my mentions blew up on Twitter—praise from my side and hate from his. Up and down my timeline, there were screenshots of his cube-shaped head next to mine. I looked crossed-eyed and crazy while yelling at that phony—safe and comfy in the studio—who claimed that I ran from the issues that plague my city. I felt as dumb as he looked. After that I decided I didn't want to do TV anymore.

Why do I need to be on camera? I thought. I was in the streets working with the kids who were responsible for the uprising. They needed real love and support from neighborhood guys like me, especially since the mayor and the president instantly wrote them off as thugs. *TV people should stick to TV,* I thought, *and I should write and do my community work.* Brandi emailed a list of shows that wanted me on the next day, while square head continued to live on my feed as my social media followers tripled. Still, I was ready to cancel all of it just to focus on working with the people who I thought needed my help the most.

When I finally got home I flopped on the couch, sparked a cig, and started flicking through some of the cable news stations. They were all covering Baltimore nonstop. Some of the reporters were trying to do good work, but many were blowing things out of proportion.

My phone buzzed and then made that annoying FaceTime sound. It was Rello. I didn't answer because I thought it was a mistake. Grown men around my way don't normally FaceTime each other—well, not dudes in their thirties.

It rung again with the same FaceTime ring so I answered.

"Man, why you take so long to answer! You too Hollywood now? We saw you on CNN cookin' boy! I'm proud of you!" he screamed. A small group of well-wishers peeked over his shoulder, forcing their way into the frame—my screen was full of gleaming lil black faces. "TV, homie, the tube! That's what I been tryin' to tell you! I told y'all that I know D. Watk!"

"Yo, for one, I find it weird that you FaceTiming me, homie. We grown men, bro," I told him. "And two, I ain't going back on TV. That clown made me lose it. I would've slapped his face off in real life!"

"Hang up, D.!" Rello said. "I'll call you on the landline."

A second later, he called back. "D., you are going back on TV, man. These streets are trashed and we need you on TV. You talking that real. You was saying the things we wanted to say, so finish your meal! Let them know how racist this dumb-ass system is, and how hard it is being black in Baltimore, man. That's your job! Finish your meal, man, finish your meal. You speakin' for us!"

Rello was right. Black representation in the media is more lopsided than Trump's hairline. But I speak for myself. There's nothing more annoying than self-appointed black voices.

TV, like print, is considered an authority—people see it and they instantly believe, and I couldn't have people believing in Bongino. I'd started something and my friends were backing me 100 percent. I now had the responsibility of being their voice—not *the* voice for every black person in America, but *a* much-needed perspective for my homies who are too often left out of the narrative. After our conversation, I went ahead and agreed to do spots and interviews at pretty much every station except Fox—and I made sure I exposed systemic racism on all of them, or at least I tried to. I like to think that I played a small role in controlling the narrative.

As time progressed, I pushed harder to play my part in controlling that black narrative. Not just by telling my story to the masses, but by setting up other writers to do the same. If some of us street guys or reformed street guys never made it to television after Gray's death, most of the mainstream media would've just painted him as a criminal who deserved to die. They paraded his arrest record as if our failed War on Drugs and racist policing wasn't to blame. They never would've mentioned how funny he was, how his community loved him, and most importantly, how he literally did nothing wrong—to date, the Baltimore Police Department has yet to provide a reason for stopping him or offer any solutions to solving the department's problem with racial profiling, meaning that it can and will happen again.

I think storytelling can bridge that divide between the department and the people or at least help make our stories heard. I don't have a monopoly on the black Baltimore perspective, and I'm not the only black writer in the city, but I am responsible for playing my part in making sure their voices resound.

I want to be a person who helps others get their voices out—creating opportunities for others is just as important as managing my own. Hopefully, I can do that for Rello and his film idea. And that, as my homie Rello puts it, is finishing my meal.

✱

THE SAD TRUTH IS BLACK LIVES REALLY DON'T MATTER

In April 2016, Terrill Thomas, a thirty-eight-year-old inmate in the Milwaukee County Jail suffering from severe mental illness, died of "profound dehydration." He spent his last days pleading—begging—for something to drink after the water in his cell was shut off. Correction officers in the jail had no problem torturing him, watching him die slowly and painfully because they did not see him as human. Thomas's death was ruled to be a homicide.

Black lives don't matter.

It was our possession. The ball was in my hands and the score was up fifteen. The game went straight to sixteen because Black Rod had winners. We were twelve years old and eager to play against Rod's sixteen-year-old friends. The game was ours: I just had to toss the ball down to Al in the post because he was stronger than everybody else. He could seamlessly turn his back on a defender and push him under the rack for an easy layup.

The play danced around in my head as I checked the rock—and then a mix of cops, uniformed and plainclothes, invaded the court from all four entrances, making all of us lie down on the ground face-first. With guns drawn on us kids, they found joy watching our noses brush concrete as they wasted our time looking for a robbery suspect. Or so they said.

Sweeps like this would continue to happen throughout my childhood. Plenty of white shirts and sneakers got ruined, along with my respect for police officers, from repeatedly being forced to lie on the ground. Those cops didn't care about our respect because they didn't see us as human.

Black lives don't matter.

The Tulsa Police Department released a video of a police officer killing Terence Crutcher in cold blood. His car stalled. He exited the vehicle for assistance, as most people in a stalled car would do, and lost his life. As requested, Crutcher had his hands up and Officer Betty Shelby still shot him.

When was the last time a white person was gunned down for needing vehicle assistance?

He was guilty of being black and didn't need a trial to prove that. Black skin is a crime and Crutcher's killer had no problem pulling the trigger because she didn't see him as human.

Black lives don't matter.

Unk-a-Bunk, or Bunk for short, used to scream suras from the Quran at the top of his lungs on the corner of Rutland Avenue. He'd pace up and down the block all day long, having an intense conversation with himself that never ended, except to invite us to his pop-up praise sessions. One day, police flooded the corner in the middle of one of Bunk's sermons.

"Shut the f*ck up! Sit your ass down!" a laughing officer said. I'm guessing Bunk's prayers interrupted his joke. That cop had been through the neighborhood plenty of times; he was a regular. He had to know that Bunk had some sort of mental illness.

"Boy, shut the f*ck up!" the cop yelled again. While Bunk sang to Allah, the officer whaled on his head with his club until he was speechless.

"Call an ambo and get this piece of sh*t to the hospital," said the officer, still laughing. Laughing was easy for him, even while a bleeding man with a disability, whom he easily could have killed, was stretched out right in front of him—because that cop didn't see Bunk as human.

Black lives don't matter.

Keith Lamont Scott, a forty-three-year-old disabled man who had a wife and seven children, was gunned down by police on a Tuesday night in Charlotte, North Carolina. Cops were serving an arrest warrant on another person and killed an innocent black man who was reportedly reading a book while waiting for his son. Brentley Vinson, the killer, was a black officer but it doesn't matter. Oppressing black people is part of his job.

Many black cops share the same mentality as racist white cops. As soon as they put on the badge, they develop the perspective embodied by Samuel L. Jackson in *Django Unchained*. The dehumanization sets in and black skin becomes illegal. Cops have to dehumanize black people as it is one of the most effective tools in administering oppression. You can't just rape, kill, and enslave people. But if they aren't people—and if they

are incapable of reason or grief, as Thomas Jefferson said—
then you can do as you please.

Black lives don't matter.

It seems like there's a new hashtag, a new video, and another
innocent black victim being murdered by police officers every
day. So much so that global threats feel like an illusion. Talk to a
black person in a predominantly black neighborhood about Al-
Qaeda or ISIS or what's happening in Syria, and they'll look at
you with the same twisted face that Libertarian candidate Gary
Johnson made when asked about Aleppo. We don't know!

Well, we do know, but it's hard for us to focus on global terrorists when domestic terrorists pin badges to their blue uniforms,
call themselves cops, and patrol our neighborhoods every day
with a license to kill. I don't know people with hero-cop stories.
Who do they model these Bruce Willis characters after?

My cop stories include murder, extortion, harassment, brutality, and disrespect on every level, and the bulk of African Americans feel the same way. Many of us feel that police officers don't
adhere to any type of moral code when dealing with black people.
Dehumanizing us allows them to function. What can we do?

We march, sing, disrupt, and protest for justice in a country
that fails to convict cops, even in cases with piles and piles of evidence. Consider Eric Garner of Staten Island, murdered on video
by an officer who used an illegal choke hold. He clearly stated
that he couldn't breathe. But to Officer Daniel Pantaleo, the cow-
ardly killer who continues to receive pay increases, Garner, like
Thomas, Crutcher, and the rest of us, wasn't human.

Black lives don't matter.

It's why we uprise.

PART 3
NEVER
PATRIOTS

10

I'M SICK OF WOKE

"Big bruh, I got these #StayWoke shirts for twenty dollars!" said the dude I've bought my incense from for over five years now. His shop is just a little ways away from my neighborhood and he always has a nice selection.

Dude bagged my goods, I paid him and proceeded to walk away as he grabbed me by the sleeve of my hoodie to show off his new merch.

"I'm good, bro," I said. "I'm not really woke!"

He laughed, "You betta wake up, man, it's a jungle out there! Stay woke!"

I shot a peace sign at him and left the store.

Everybody's woke now, right? I wonder how that's working out?

The term "woke" simply refers to not being asleep, not being ignorant to the issues that plague black America—racism, poor schools, food deserts, crooked cops, our broken justice system, unfair hiring practices, and the banks that bury us with vicious Black Taxes like unfair interest rates on mortgages. You know . . . the hurdles.

Woke people know the origins of everything that hurts black people, the policies that allow these systems to function, and have

the most effective language when given the opportunity to explain these issues, mainly online or during the intermission at spoken-word readings. Woke people are smart—they are normally educated with at least one bachelor's degree, keep a copy of a James Baldwin or bell hooks book on their person, have a passport, are fluent in all forms of social media, and have been to Cuba at least once since Obama lifted the embargo.

Woke people wear locs or baby fros and use coconut oil, olive oil, and hemp soap. They blog, they have a brand, they wrap themselves in henna or war paint at festivals even though they rarely engage in a physical war, if they ever engage at all.

Woke people have the best graphic T-shirts and catchiest hashtags. They have great jobs or no job because their families can afford to float them, they are the first to pop up at a protest, take the best viral images, and run home to talk about it on the internet. Sharing variations of the same image repeatedly. Here are some of my favorites:

- Group selfie at the protest
- Screaming at a cop they'd never touch
- Definitely that iconic image where a small group does the black power fist pump
- Solo image doing the black power fist pump
- And if you are lucky, you'll get that newsworthy clip of yourself being arrested, shouting "fight the power" as you go off to be detained for three hours

I went to two protests before I realized they weren't for me. The woke crowd seemed off and I didn't know why. I guess it felt like everybody was talking to a group of people who don't listen. It wasn't until Donald Stevenson, a real activist sitting in the audience at a panel I sat on in Southeast DC, broke it down that I understood.

I shared the stage with two well-known authors and community leaders, reentry expert Tony Lewis Jr. and artist Aaron Maybin. We were talking about our community work to a small crowd, sharing successes and failures and telling people what they could do to help us if they wanted to be a part of the positive changes happening in DC and Baltimore, beyond protests. It was light, funny, and I think some people were inspired. Then this loudmouth dude in a linty sweater and wide-leg dress pants barged in yelling, "Y'all Black Lives Matter people not gonna be coming to my neighborhood and telling me how to run it!"

I laughed to keep from flipping out on the dude. My temper had got the best of me on a panel before and I didn't want to embarrass myself or the organizers.

"Aye, man, you owe us an apology. You know who I am and the work I do," Tony said. "We all work together to make DC better for everybody and these brothers are doing great work in Baltimore, so sit down. You sound silly!"

Dress-pants guy became real humble real fast—I couldn't stop laughing. But his anger sparked a bigger conversation about the black narrative in general.

A woman in the front row shifted the conversation. "Y'all only talk about police murder, what about all this black-on-black crime, that's the real problem! Black lives don't matter when we kill our own!"

Donald Stevenson responded from the audience:

Protesting has always been the response of middle-class African Americans to injustices. A response that takes a great deal of strategic planning, resources, and education on various issues. Black Lives Matter isn't any different. While on the contrary, the response of poorer African Americans is more in-your-face direct and oftentimes referred to as hostile resistance or abrupt disorderly conduct.

One asked, "Where is the outcry when blacks kill other blacks?" Well, let me show you. It can be found within the countless murals (sidewalk and wall) found in the black community; the countless trees lined with teddy bears and liquor bottles; the hostility toward police in the community who are sworn to protect and serve and who are always present except at the time of many violent attacks. It can be seen in the overflow of emotion at funerals of slain young people; and, due to the lack of positive safe outlets for grief and loss counseling and the miseducation of effective coping mechanisms, will often lead to self-medication to suppress these emotions. Leading to high rates of drug abuse and alcoholism. I can go on and on. So honestly, all the "Woke People," aka Poverty/Struggle Pimps, exit left.

Let's coin a new phrase: "get active." To be "woke" for most African Americans, to me, is the equivalent of "white guilt." It's usually thrown around by the offspring of black elites, either Ivy League or prestigious HBCU grads, individuals who have no consistent ties to inner-city African American communities, where many of the issues they take pride in fighting for are simply the everyday reality for those who have no other choice but to endure.

He summed it up. Everything I was thinking in one response and it validated my experience. I instantly saw images of this funeral I attended for a friend named Baggy a week prior—dude was twenty-three and it was packed wall to wall—aunts and grannies crying, people throwing up and passing out. Tears on every face.

Stevenson's point made me think about the middle- and upper middle–class African Americans unable to understand the poor and vice versa. We speak differently, but society puts us in the same group because of our skin color. As always, the more affluent get the opportunity to control the narrative, so being "woke" is hot and will be until the rest of black America gets a voice.

Now I have a book out and I'm a voice. I travel, meet "woke" people all of the time, and tell them that they are a voice—not *the* voice but *a* voice—but that doesn't mean much for the betterment of our people if action is not added to those words.

ONE BLACK VOICE

A nonprofit booked me to speak to some young writers from Baltimore.

"How does it feel to be the voice of the people?" a giggly girl in cat-eye frames asked.

"I don't speak for all of black America," I told her. "I'm not the voice of black Baltimore, or Down Da Hill, or Latrobe Housing Projects, The Avenue, or any other section of the city. I'm just one guy."

The group shrugged in confusion.

I have to say that over and over again, every time I do an event or appear on one of these TV, podcast, or radio shows. Don't get me wrong, I love representing my people and my city. I try to do so with the utmost respect. But we need to move beyond the idea of there being one black voice. I don't know people like Cornel West, Al Sharpton, or Tavis Smiley, and they definitely can't speak for me. Maybe they can articulate some of the issues that affect black America in a negative way, but that doesn't make one an authority on the black experience and many of the people who live in poverty are not really listening to them anyway—you need Wi-Fi or cable to get their messages. We know that Jennifer Lopez isn't the only Latina, and we don't assume David Duke and Tom Brady share the same ideas just because their skin color is the same. So why does there have to be one black voice?

I don't study policy and hang around city hall, so why does my voice matter more than the African Americans that have mastered those things? Because I have more followers? I spend my free time in the street. My little homie Nick, a thirteen-year-old, needed a couple dollars and some guidance to keep him away from selling smack. I stepped in, provided that cash, and told him, "Selling dope looks cool, man, but it's not. The streets lead to two places: death or the pen. Trust me."

The fact is that there are so many black people in America doing great work, with their personal stories of redemption, ideas, and ways to be effective. How corny would it be for me to try and take all the credit? It's exactly how corny it is when other people try to do it.

I've been fortunate enough to meet so many amazing people who are doing work that really matters. These people are leaders in their own right, with their own ideas and agendas. I'm sure we wouldn't agree on everything and that's cool, but again, the idea isn't to propel one holy black anointed person as the chosen one, but for all of us to reach mastery at what we do, work together, share those skills, and support each other. Even though I don't personally identify as an activist, I understand that activism has many faces.

I had a conversation about this very topic with a lawyer friend of mine who works with young activists.

"A young guy that hits all of these protests told me that he didn't respect anybody in a suit! Can you believe that? As if we are the problem," he laughingly said. "I told him that us suits are the ones who go downtown to get the permits that keep you young guys out of jail when you organize these marches. And if you do get arrested, we suits get you out!"

Everyone must do his or her part if we really want change. The age of having one black leader is over, as it should be. It's hard enough to get a group of five to agree on something as simple as dinner, let alone the direction of an entire race.

I hope the idea catches on. We must move beyond the "black box" that marginalizes what our experiences are, or what they can be. If we can successfully do that, a new wave of black voices will flourish and social relations will enhance drastically.

We'll set quantifiable goals, accomplish them, move beyond yelling "woke," and start living the lives we truly deserve.

11

ARE YOU A REAL ONE?

Brooklyn.

It's a magical place for many—full of life, art, community, and rich experiences. It represents none of these things to me. I just go there to collect checks.

Therefore, who could have been happier than I was leaving a boring meeting with some boring people at a forgettable restaurant in Fort Greene.

I exploded out the door into a breezy New York afternoon, their phony good-byes and "We'll be in touch, D.!" following me out.

Rewind:

I walked in an hour early, as I always walk in an hour early—old hustler trick. Being early to meetings allows me to survey the spot and pick the seat facing the door so that I can see them enter and have them walk toward me as if I called the meeting. I can pick out their chairs and make it so their backs face the door—even though that probably won't make them uneasy because it seems like nothing does. See, they are young, they are woke, they are white, and they are in Brooklyn, which is why they are fearless. Not speaking for all white people, but you catch my drift.

"Is that D. Watkins?!" Mitch said, walking in. "OHHHHH, ohhhhhhh, rocking the Air Max 97s! All praise to the most high! I see you, bro!" He waved his hands up and down like a grandma midway through the sermon.

Mitch is a stick with shoulders, his vintage Carhartt jacket looked like it was floating toward me. Vintage jeans, vintage hat, vintage specs—just like the rest of the twenty-three-year-old suburban New York transplants at these magazines who've mastered black culture more than me.

"D., bro, I can't believe you are walking around BK with those bright shoes. They are gonna get soooo cooked!"

I laughed.

Mitch is not officially with *Vice* or A&E or any of the other networks he's said he's pitching a show based on my life to. We met after one of my readings in New York and he promised to help take my career to the next level.

"Where is your partner?" I asked.

He ordered a quad-shot latte. "Bro, you are going to love Robin. She's so plugged: MTV, VH1, Gucci, XXL, BET, and everyone else, bro. She's an industry darling!"

I always get scared when I hear people throw around credentials. I'm not from Missouri, but show me some results. I held my laugh in. With all the name-dropping, I wasn't sure if I was in Brooklyn or L.A.

"Hiiiiii guys!" said a woman version of Mitch. "You must be D.!"

I reached for a handshake. "No, no D.! I'm a hugger!"

I cuffed my shoulders, giving her that business-friendly church hug. Robin dived deep into conversation, asking me what I wanted and then telling me what I needed to be doing—how to act, present myself, and what it meant to be black. An abstract

ARE YOU A REAL ONE? **109**

picture of Biggie stared down at us from the walls of a modern café as two white people told me—a black person with thirty-plus-years' experience of being black, who grew up in an all-black neighborhood in an all-black city—what it meant to black.

Mobb Deep played on the speaker and they instantly stopped explaining blackness so that they could reflect on the golden age of hip hop and the Queensbridge housing projects—a place they'd never been—in a similar fashion to the German philosopher Immanuel Kant's views on Africa.

"Yo, y'all should read my essays and pitch some ideas to your people," I said, fake checking my phone as if I had missed phone calls and emails. "Hit me up when it's time to talk money!"

I blasted out of the door. Left, right, and straight ahead, these streets all looked the same to me: gentrified. I didn't really know which direction to head—toward the café or toward the café. So, like most non–New Yorkers, I whipped out my iPhone and punched the Lyft app. My driver was four minutes away.

"Is that Lil Dwight?" yelled an older guy in a puffy Army coat and a new Yankees cap with a tilted brim, stickers still on. "Lil Dwight, D. Watk! What it do, baby boy?"

I squinted as he walked closer. His New York accent was heavier than his husky frame.

"O.G.! What's up, homie?!" I yelled back.

"It's been like ten years, duke!" he replied, dapping me twice and then pulling me in for a bear hug.

The Lyft driver pulled up. "O.G., hop in this cab with me!"

"Nah, duke! I'm from Brooklyn, I ain't with those funny cabs, man. Take a walk with ya uncle, though. My spot up da block!"

Up the block to a New Yorker could be sixty miles; but it's O.G., so I had to roll.

＊✳＊

O.G. is Brooklyn—old Brooklyn, an original, not one of these transplants. You know: the tradition erasers, the Christopher Columbus types who swoop in, force rents to rise, and start naming and claiming the blocks as their own, as if they were born there with roots that sink five generations deep. His mom didn't name him O.G., but he is one.

"I saw you on TV, duke!" he said, biting the plastic wrapper off of a Black & Mild and spitting it out. "You really brought B-more to CNN, raw as hell too! It brought back hella memories! I was like, that's my lil nigga! Salute da God! Man, my roomies kept sayin', 'You don't know him.'"

I met O.G. back in the early 2000s. He was that loud Brooklyn dude on the basketball court who never missed an opportunity to tell you he was from Brooklyn. You've met this guy before: "I don't call foul; I'm from Brooklyn! And one, count the bucket; I'm from Brooklyn! That's my ball! Give it up; I'm from Brooklyn!"

"But you just said you don't call fouls?"

"Now I do, because I'm from Brooklyn!"

Those rants on the court got him into a bunch of fights. Sometimes he won, sometimes he got stomped out, but he always came back, and that's how he earned the respect of so many people from the neighborhood, because just like the old Brooklyn, we're always down to go thirty rounds.

"I'm tellin' you, Lil Dwight—I mean D. Watk—my brothas I stay with were saying I don't know you! We watched all of that wild riot stuff in B-more and you just kept popping up," O.G. said. "My man's daughter is reading your book for school and everything. They're gonna flip when we hit the crib."

"Hell no, for real?"

"Yeah man, for real! I don't lie; I'm from Brooklyn!"

We strolled through a bunch of random blocks, the kind that make up the new Brooklyn, full of trash-sorting, bun-wearing, bearded men who all dress the same: dark designer frames, flannels or thrift sweaters, and cuffed skinnies with crazy-print socks over Air Jordans, Red Wing boots, shell-toe Adidas, or worn-out Stan Smiths. The trash-sorting women dress mostly the same, except for the ones who look like they buy their clothes from the closet of a '90s drug dealer: Moschino tees, big Coogi sweaters, Air Force 1s, and bomber coats. (Imagine a skinny, twenty-year-old white girl in Park Slope auditioning to play a goon in a Nas video from '94.)

"You rich yet, lil homie? Out here grabbing a funny cab when you should be in a limo—you rich and cheap?" O.G. asked. I laughed even though he was dead serious.

"Hell no, I'm not rich!" I said. "Don't let TV fool you, bro."

"Well, you should be rich! Not saying this 'cause you my lil homie, saying it because the news stay hiring these whitewashed fake people, and you came live from the gutta," he replied. "Let a real one like me manage you, we'll get to the paper!"

He dapped me again. O.G. is old Brooklyn, so every conversation comes with a sixty-handshake minimum.

We banged a left onto Flatbush, catching up on everything from sports to mutual friends in federal prison to our own little episode of *Where Are They Now? East Baltimore Edition*. It went something like "He's dead, he's in jail, she finished college, he's dead, and they joined church."

O.G. had just come off a ten-year bid three years ago. Catching federal time was easy back in the early 2000s. Black dudes were being slapped with ten years just because their names were popping up in conversations about drug crews. Imagine being flat broke and being charged as a kingpin.

O.G.'s crib was on Chauncey Street in Bedford-Stuyvesant. A light-skinned guy with a skinny beard, built and dressed similarly to O.G., sat on the steps. "Yo, Fox! Look who I found, B.!" O.G. said, reaching out to him for a handshake.

Fox squinted. "Oh yooo, bro, what's good? Let me go get Turk!" he said, shaking my hand with both of his, presidential style. "His daughter's reading your stuff for class! We really got a book writer in the hood!"

"Yo, I'm an article writer too!" I laughed.

Fox went inside. I posted up out front with O.G. He pulled a Black & Mild out from behind his ear and sparked it. Mostly black and brown people passed us as we sat out front. Every once in a while, a white jogger with an iPhone arm strap ran by—a key indicator that Bed-Stuy is prepping to be the next Fort Greene.

"I met Fox in the joint, he was a wild gunslinger back in the day," said O.G., passing me the Black & Mild. "His cousin Turk got a rich church uncle that owns this crib. He lets us rent it for cheap. Not sure how long before he wanna flip and make a money play. Man, everybody else doing it."

Fox and another guy came out of the house and joined us on the steps. "Oh, big homie! We got a writer on the block! Salute, fam! I'm Turk," the other guy said. "My daughter's class is reading your book up in Washington Heights, D.! I ain't read it yet, but if it's anything like O.G. say about B-more, I know it's raw!"

My friend Antoine, who's also from Baltimore, lives in New York now and is an administrator at a middle school way uptown near 170th Street. He worked hard to get the school to purchase one hundred copies of my first book, *The Beast Side*, and we were planning an assembly for the students later on that school year. Turk's daughter was one of those students.

"Man, I try to be real with the kids," I said. "I hope she likes it."

Turk dipped in the crib and came back out with three plastic cups and a fifth of Hennessy. "Gotta do some shots with the writer! They don't come around here. Never! Watkins, you a real one!"

"Nah, there's writers around here for sure. They just don't really care about us," Fox interrupted. "All these white people with the laptop bags, all these people in glasses—man, somebody's writing something!"

We all laughed.

I took a long pull of the Black & Mild—the longest—inhaling the smoke until the ashes almost burned the plastic tip. "Yo, honestly, I'd feel like a clown if I wasn't able to sit anywhere and be comfortable in my own skin," I said.

O.G. agreed, holding a cigarillo in his left hand while slicing it down the center with his right index finger, allowing blunt guts to sprinkle out, dusting over his tattered Timbs and the cuffs in his boot-cut jeans. Old Brooklyn.

Turk filled our cups, and we toasted: "To being real ones."

"Being a real one" or "keepin' it real" are terms that are tossed around, but not accurately—the reason being is that most aren't real. Everyone claims to be "real" or wants to be but often fails to meet the simple requirements.

O.G. and his friends calling me "real" was more about my accessibility and how we engaged than me guzzling a cup full of Hennessy in an unfamiliar neighborhood, acting super tough, or claiming to be "gangsta"—as these are things that I don't do. Most tend to tie being a real one to these actions in addition to doing hard drugs, fighting for no real reason, never putting the toilet seat down, and all other forms of hypermasculinity, but this is false.

You can act like a thug and be just as fake as the criminals who commit crimes and save themselves by snitching on other criminals. And vice versa, take the black guy who comes into the hood and brags about being the only black guy on his job—never trying to help anyone else from the neighborhood get hired. They made it, white people love them, they learned how to play golf, and that's enough for them to die happy.

I used to play basketball twice a week at Johns Hopkins University in the student, faculty, and employee game. There was this medium built, curly headed West Baltimore dude named Joey that basically owned the gym—no, he didn't have a deed to the property, but he could hit shots from anywhere on the court as if it were his home. It didn't matter if you pushed him, kicked his leg, or hung from his arm, his shots would fall—dude was easily the best player in attendance every week. I never really had a problem with him, but some of the guys in the gym did, mainly because Joey ran his mouth and talked too much trash, like most twentysomething non-pros with freakish talent.

One day he walked into the gym with a heavy face and addressed a couple of us on the sideline, "Sup fellas, I really need a job, man," he said. "Do y'all know of any spot that's hiring? I'll do anything, I just want to take care of my kids."

A grad student and I exchanged numbers with him as I was in between jobs myself at the time and figured we could work together on finding employment. One of the black professors sitting near us popped up, shrugged, and yelled, "Split the teams up, guys! I'm ready to play!"

The professor and Joey ended up on opposite sides, and as usual, Joey put on a show, shooting his lights out, making half of his baskets from two or three steps behind the three-point line. Toward the end of the game, Joey called a foul on the professor. The professor didn't agree and it turned into a huge argument between the two. A few of us stepped in and mediated, but the professor quit the game saying, "I should never have to argue with a person like you. I'm a Johns Hopkins professor and you can't even find a job!" We all looked at him like he'd lost his mind as he stormed out.

"Damn, I just made a call," said Joey. "I didn't know that he would attack my personal life!"

Now, don't be fooled, this black professor also looked the part—see, he dressed like a person who many would identify as a real one. He had a Nas fade, Air Jordans, and even a little gold chain, but it was all a façade. The professor, like many, loved to look like the dudes from the hood, act like they are from the hood, and use that brash ghetto bravado when it pays dividends, but will reject any- and everything black when a real hood dude walks in the room or they get the opportunity to gain white validation.

That professor is not alone, as these incidents have happened to me all over the publishing world. Imagine owning a bank full of hood quotes, perks, and experiences that you can draw from whenever you want and never have to deposit anything into it, you don't even have to acknowledge it. There are plenty of writers; reverends; street dudes; pin-and-button-heavy backpack, Air Jordan nerds; fro-patting soul sistas; and down brothas who use words like "cisgender" and "intersectionality." They flex their identity, screaming "I'm unapologetically black" until their lungs pop. They apply full pressure to conservatives and white liberals in the name of the people, but they don't really know the people, outside of other famous entertainers, tweeters, and public figures.

Kiss up to your fellow stars, but disrespect the black limo driver when he misses a turn and scream at the black waitress when she makes a mistake and puts ice in your water as if she's supposed to notice that you wear scarves indoors and instantly know you'd prefer room temperature. You get to escape to your cul-de-sac and figure out more ways to profit from their real pain while doing absolutely nothing to enhance the black experience in America. Your #StayWoke tees, sponsored rallies, and speaking gigs are not feeding anybody but you. These people are the reason I struggle with representation.

HOW CAN YOU SPEAK FOR ME IF YOU DON'T KNOW ANYONE LIKE ME?

Everybody is running around screaming "Freddie Gray! Trayvon Martin! Michael Brown! Sandra Bland!," but did they know them? Do they socialize with people like them? The real question is: Could Freddie Gray have called you if he needed a recommendation for a job? The whole world wants justice for Freddie now, but it wasn't worried about justice for him when he was alive and out here trying to make it. The same goes for Michael Brown in Ferguson. Could Brown reach out to you if he needed help finding college scholarships or advice on interview etiquette? Would you shake Trayvon Martin's hand? Really, would you? Because I know royal TV show hosts, writers who cover these issues, and activists who have zero proximity to real people—they can't touch real people from their ivory tower, so they don't really understand the issues beyond shock-value stats and talking points. This is why the same systemic injustices have lingered since my parents' parents were kids.

Do you really want to keep it real? Having a community presence is the first step toward understanding. Venture into the spots and spend time with the people you'd like to help. Teach them how you achieved your goals as a professional artist, journalist, or lawyer so that we continue to grow and strengthen the black community. Be available: don't brag about being the only minority in your office, put somebody else in there. What's more valuable than a mentor that you can call, see, or touch?

An alternative to the professor I described above is the writer Wes Moore. Wes is talented and accomplished, doesn't try to dress to like anyone other than himself, and helps people. Instead of playing hood, he helps young people from the hood work toward gaining the same type of success that he enjoys.

Contrary to what many believe, black people don't want handouts. In case you forgot, our ancestors built this country through brutal and harsh slave labor. We just want a fair shake like everyone else.

It's a running joke in our community that we have to work twenty times as hard to achieve the same success that other races enjoy. Hopkins professor Karl Alexander proved many of those jokes true when he published *The Long Shadow*, a thirty-five-year study showing that whites with jail records and higher reported drug use still had more opportunities than squeaky-clean African Americans who had attended college. But we already knew this. I'll never expect a level playing field in this country. But if you care, and want to do something like many "real ones" proclaim, please be a mentor or a resource to somebody. Live in the tradition of Frederick Douglass and Harriet Tubman.

Once Douglass and Tubman became free, they dedicated their lives to freeing other black people, and that's real. Not enough of the go-to voices of modern movements are helping other black people. I believe, however, that this can change, and that's the primary reason I'd rather directly address my people than make another plea to the dominant culture. Somehow, the smartest minority minds still don't understand that the oppressors don't listen.

If oppressors listened or considered your feelings, they wouldn't be oppressors.

✳

PEOPLE FROM THE HOOD DON'T NORMALLY PUT IT IN THEIR BIO

My young homie Kondwani listens to J. Cole and wears a nose ring. He works at a bookshop, where he spends his free time writing poetry, reading Toni Morrison, and studying the writings of Ibram X. Kendi. He guzzles quad-shot oat milk lattes and attempts to be vegan every few months. He's also an MFA student in the most historically white discipline: creative writing. He's not like the rest of them.

But he really is. See, Kondwani is from the hood. Down Da Hill, like me, where they aren't really debating Morrison, studying Kendi, drinking oat milk, or paying seven dollars for a coffee—or at least that's the narrative that's normally told, and it's not true, as he proudly does all of these things. I've hung around Kondwani hundreds of times, and I've never heard him scream "I'm from the hood!," because people from the hood never do.

I wasn't even aware that being from the hood was a thing that people bragged about until I had some experiences outside of my community. I love my neighborhood, where I come from and where I still am, as it is responsible for me being me. However, people take it too far.

"I am the hood! Real talk, da hood!" I heard an angry guy yell on the basketball court at Hopkins. "G-Dawg, bro! Ask about me!" He was thin, black, in his late twenties, almost six foot, and completely wrapped in Under Armour—headband, arm sleeve, tank, dude even had the socks.

"I hear you, Slim," I said, making my way to the sideline and loosening my knee brace.

I don't argue with Hopkins kids about basketball games for a number of reasons: I'm out of shape, I'm an old professor, and they talk really tough, all the way up until you punch them. Punch a Hopkins student and they hit back by calling the cops and pressing maximum charges. I guess I know this because I'm from the hood.

"I will beat they ass!" G-Dawg said, joining me on the sideline. We were playing on the same team, and he and I had just lost bad. G-Dawg made some questionable calls, but I rode with him because that's what good teammates do. He continued to ramble: more tough talk, so much that his gangsta-isms seeped through my noise-reduction headphones. I took them off to hear him out. He was funny.

A spindly grad student I've known for years walked in. He evidently knew G-Dawg well and greeted him with a bear hug—one of those tight embraces where both parties rock back and forth.

"Hey, Gregory!" the student said, letting go of G-Dawg. "How are you? How are your parents?" he continued, patting G-Dawg on the shoulder.

"Everybody is swell. God, it feels like ages, bro. I think about camp all of the time," replied G-Dawg—or Gregory, I guess.

Swell, I thought to myself. *Who says swell?* Gregory was not like the rest of them.

Gregory went on to talk about his research and then made some references to a guy named Dave Matthews and a bunch of stuff I'd never heard of. I swear, this was the best display of code-switching I'd ever seen in my life. He was the Michael Jordan of code-switching. Dude deserves medals, a grant, or something.

For those who don't know, code-switching is when black people abandon the vernacular, ditch any trace of colloquial sound, harden the "r"s in words that end in "r," and say "actually" before every comment in an effort to be understood by white people. G-Dawg and Gregory sounded like two different people.

The grad student greeted me next. Gregory, or G-Dawg, jumped on with a team I didn't want to play with and I stretched in preparation for the next game.

"We gonna win for sure, Watkins," the grad student said. He asked me about work and I asked him about G-Dawg. They had attended private school together from grades six through twelve. G-Dawg grew up in a two-parent household in Montgomery, one of the most affluent counties in the country.

So where does this gangsta act come from? Do societal factors push black men into these hypermasculine behaviors? Don't cry, be extra tough, cuss everyone out on the court, and always mask your pain, heartache, and love—these behaviors are definitely reinforced in music and in the way we are portrayed in the media and on television. This causes two major issues.

The first deals with the street-dealing stereotype that gets applied to all men from the hood. Kondwani, the young man I mentioned earlier, is intelligent, comfortable in his own skin, and couldn't care less about being seen as a "super thug" because he's not one. There are plenty of dudes from the hood who love manga, skateboards, Pokémon, comic books, and can quote Dave Matthews (I Googled him). Only people who are really from the hood know this.

The other issue comes from dudes like G-Dawg who are constantly forced to buy into that stereotype.

I don't know his life. Maybe he spent his weekends in the projects or something, but the idea of him feeling like he has to proclaim that is a problem. It doesn't matter if you're from the hood or the burbs—no one deserves to be disrespected. However, acting like a gangsta who is exempt from disrespect only creates more fearful people, such as cops who see guys from the hood as automatically dangerous, so they aim and fire after three-minute interactions, or judges who see stereotypes and not people, so they easily give us unfair sentences.

I am not blaming street culture on systemic racism, as racism existed long before fake thugs. But not everybody from the hood is a gangsta, so let's change that false narrative and stop playing gangsta to get respect. It doesn't work, especially when a real gangsta walks into the room.

MEETING A REAL ONE

I must've appeared to be a *good one*, or not like the rest of them to somebody, because I was invited to meet President Barack Obama. Well, not a one-on-one like Steph Curry or Kendrick Lamar, but an invitation to be in the same room. Here's the email:

Good morning:

Here are all the details for the ABC prime-time special with President Obama.

The venue is:

14th & P street NW, Studio Theater
Washington D.C.

The special will start taping at about 2:30 pm or 3 pm, so we are asking all guests to arrive at the theater by 12:45 pm for security clearance.

We will tape the conversation for about an hour.

For Secret Service clearance, could you please provide the following information as soon as possible:

> Legal name (as it appears on driver's license)
> Date of Birth
> SSN
> Country of Citizenship
> Gender
> Country of Birth
> City and State of Residence (as it appears on driver's license)
> Email
> Cell Phone

Please let me know if you have any questions or concerns. Thanks very much.

I couldn't believe it. Me, a dude from the streets, being in the same room as the first black president. Let me put this into perspective. When Obama gave his breakout speech in 2004 at the Democratic National Convention, I was knee-deep in a dope hole—serving fiends, ducking the law, and trying not to get my brains blown out.

I was in college in 2008 when people started rambling about this black guy who was smoother than silk and had the infrastructure needed to become the first black president. Then I heard his name, Barack Hussein Obama, and went, "Hell no! Not in racist America. That's the name of a dude who sells incense and oils, not a president."

Obama won Iowa, which plenty of people thought was impossible. For the first time in my life, I witnessed people in my neighborhood believing in someone; believing in the government and feeling that it can work for us.

I started following the campaign on CNN, MSNBC, and Fox News. It was the first campaign I had ever followed, and I can honestly say Obama changed my life. He *really* wasn't like the rest of them. The way he carried himself not only made me want to be a better person, but challenged me to do so. And when he won, I knew I had to win as well in my own way. I even started wearing khakis and sweater vests for no reason.

Nothing really changed in my neighborhood after he was elected—some of my friends who were inspired and changed their lives around ended up being gunned down in the same streets where we'd celebrated his victory. RIP Free, Bags, and Scola. Not saying it's Obama's fault, but we learned the hard way that it takes more than one black president to erase hundreds of years of systemic racism and societal ills; however, I still remembered that 2008 Obama feeling, and I was excited to meet him.

"The President and the People" was the name of the town

hall. The hour-long special was moderated by David Muir, and was intended to be a dialogue between the president and the citizens who are suffering the most from our more-than-obvious problem with race and law enforcement.

I put creases in the sleeves of my polo and got to the venue an hour early.

The ABC producer who invited me said that I'd get the chance to ask the president a question, to help elicit a better understanding of how the federal government plans to deal with these issues. I wanted to ask the president why he went to Dallas, where five police officers were murdered, but didn't come to Baltimore, which is just down the highway from his home, or to Ferguson, Baton Rouge, Albuquerque, Oakland, or any of the cities where the streets have been smeared with innocent black blood.

The killings in Dallas were tragic, but aren't they all?

The studio mirrored a viral internet video convention, everybody that lived on my timeline was present, from Officer Nakia Jones to Philando Castile's girlfriend Diamond Reynolds, appearing on a huge monitor. The room was full of activists, selfie-takers, and cops. I saw enough faces familiar from TV to realize I wasn't cable news or internet famous enough to speak, but it didn't matter because one of these passionate people would get the chance to ask the president a tough question.

I was wrong.

The first mistake was the silly lieutenant governor of Texas, Dan Patrick, who used his chance to ask a question to pompously try to chastise the president for his response to the killing of the police officers, as if Obama hadn't instantly made a statement, traveled to Dallas, presided over a memorial service for the fallen officers, and hugged their spouses and children. Nothing is good enough for people like Patrick, whose only beef with Obama was his political affiliation and the color of his skin.

Young to middle-aged black men are the main ones being gunned down by police officers, but none of us got a chance to say one word. We heard from two black children: Cameron Sterling, the son of Alton Sterling—the black man whose death at the hands of police officers in Baton Rouge sparked nationwide protest—bravely spoke, and so did a college student and Black Lives Matter activist from Ferguson. The closest person to the targeted demographic to speak was Coffey Anderson, a thirty-eight-year-old black country singer from Texas, whose career, ideology, and style of dress don't really represent most of those being gunned down during routine traffic stops. I never saw a victim of police brutality in a ten-gallon hat and spurred cowboy boots.

The rest of the questions and comments came from a few women who were victims of police violence. They complained about white men acting as if they were the victims. There was also the mother of a police officer who feared for her son's safety because he was hit with a water bottle while patrolling during the Baltimore Uprising. Yeah, a water bottle.

More disturbingly, the mother of Michael Slager, the cop who murdered Walter Scott in cold blood and then lied about the whole incident in his police report, was acknowledged as being in the crowd, as if anyone cared, but Gwen Carr and Erica Garner, the mother and daughter of Eric Garner, were not.

Erica dedicated her life to activism after her father died from an illegal choke hold administered by a coward—New York City police officer Daniel Pantaleo. Though Pantaleo's choke hold and Eric Garner's cries of "I can't breathe!" were caught on tape, a grand jury declined to indict.

She sat a couple rows ahead of me and made the same twisted facial expressions as me in response to some of the things that came out of Obama's mouth, like how it was hard to indict cops because they are here to help us. Help who? Maybe you, but not us.

So, what do we do if Barack Obama—one of the most intelligent people on the planet, smoother than silk, and the only man talented enough to become an African American president—refuses to have a real conversation about the role of race in policing?

Garner and I were both upset by the remarks made by the president, specifically how he spoke about police violence. I was even more upset that she didn't get a chance to speak. Her dad's death focused international attention on the issue of police brutality against black Americans, and she had traveled all the way from New York to DC because she was promised a chance to address the president. Why should I think my black life matters when I get invited to a show about our country's race problem, and people like the Garner family, who have suffered more than most, aren't even given the time of day?

Garner stormed out of the room, letting everyone have it, including the Secret Service. Ultimately, she was given the opportunity to speak with the President in private, where she told him how she really felt. She didn't kiss up to him or beg to take a picture with him, like many self-proclaimed change agents do; she gave him the hard facts about what black people were really going through all over the country at the time and challenged him to do something about her father's death.

We traveled back to the train station together. "That town hall was horrible," Erica said. "He phony, talking about politics and this Trump stuff. I wasn't trying to hear it. I wasted my time coming down here!"

She continued, talking about police violence and the problems with modern activism. Erica got it. She was extremely intelligent, funny, raw, and understood the issues. I'm sorry that the death of her father brought her into activism, but I'm blessed to have had the chance to meet her. Many were put off by her actions at the studio, but I was inspired. She was the type of leader we needed in our communities, in government, and representing us in the media: A person who bathes in honesty and is not scared to speak truth to power. A person who will call BS when she sees it, even at the highest level.

And sadly, we lost her at the end of 2017. That same pain she addressed ABC with caused her to have a heart attack at the age of twenty-seven.

Erica Garner spoke from the heart. She didn't use opportunities like books and interviews to push false narratives; rather, she gave us the truth in a sobering way that's key to creating the change we'd like to see. She'll be forever missed.

I started that day excited to meet Obama, but the win was meeting Erica. She's a real one.

RIP sis, love you.

12

INTELLECTUALLY CURIOUS OR RACIST?

I don't jump out there and tell people not to be racist. I don't even really argue with racists, write love letters to white people about their privilege, or tell them to "be better." I'm not against people who do. It just doesn't seem like the best use of my time.

You see, there are two types of white people. There are the ones who are intellectually curious and there are the ones who really don't care. You don't have to sing or write love letters to the intellectually curious because they are curious, they want to learn—so the conversation looks more like an exchange of ideas rather than an argument full of insensitive language. The ones who really don't care—the Sean Hannity lovers, the Rush Limbaugh listeners, and the Klan-wannabe tiki torch clowns—are not worth the energy. However, one question I keep coming back to again and again is: It's 2019, so why can't we have a *real* conversation about race? I have asked myself this question often over the last year. It frequently finds its way into my social settings, uninvited and annoying, like that pebble in your running sneaker.

"Can I start you off with a drink?" asked the bartender in a near-empty restaurant across from the campus where I teach. I was celebrating the end of the semester. I had just marked a zillion papers and entered final grades—some As, a lot of Bs, a couple Cs, and even three Fs.

"A glass of champagne? Vodka mixed with champagne? Anything mixed with champagne?" I replied.

The guy next to me laughed, dropping his book onto the floor. I reached down, picked it up, and handed it to him.

"Thank you," he said. "I love your drink choices. You're my kind of guy!"

He was white, spikey haired, thin, and wore small frameless rectangle glasses, you know, the kind accountants wear. But dude also looked like a coach or an Old Navy model, all fleeced and zipped.

We then had a random exchange about Baltimore sports, Baltimore holidays, and Baltimore politics—all laughs, a black guy and a white guy both irritated by the same BS—Dr. King's dream was in full effect.

A former student of mine, Mia, from another college I taught at, walked in with a few friends. They sat on the three empty stools directly to the right of us.

"Professor Watkins!" Mia yelled. "Your next drink is on us—even though you gave me a B+. You know you could've gave me an A!"

We all laughed.

"He a professor?" one of Mia's friends asked. "He looks like a student, right?"

The white guy, who happened to be the only white guy at the bar besides the bartender, nudged me.

"That's a real honor," the white guy said. "I can't believe you are a professor, man. Wow, congrats."

I wasn't sure why he couldn't believe it, or why Mia's friend was so shocked either, but I didn't really care to press the issue. I had just graded two zillion papers and was trying to enjoy my gentrified champagne cocktail.

"Watkins!" Mia said. "You ever been to the Belvedere? They got two really nice bars over there."

"Yeah, but the Belvedere is racist!" I laughed. "I stopped going in there after I saw how they did my man Mos Def in that HBO flick."

The movie I referenced was *Something the Lord Made*, a biopic about a black doctor named Vivien Thomas who performed revolutionary work at Johns Hopkins Hospital but went most of his career without receiving recognition, and even had to work as a server at the Belvedere while practicing medicine. In one scene, he was denied entrance into a Belvedere event that all of his colleagues had been invited to and was forced to use the service entrance. I was joking about not going to the Belvedere, as racist institutions, or institutions with a racist past, are all over the country. White guy wasn't amused.

"So, was that in 1940 or 2016? I don't understand why you are calling the place racist. Racism is over," the white guy said, slamming down his cup. He had started to raise his voice, but then he caught himself.

"I was joking, man," I said. "I really wasn't talking to you, and I honestly don't care about that place. And mentioning the racist legacy of a place is legal, right?"

Mia chimed in, discussing her graduate school experiences and some of the issues she had been facing dealing with race. As an older guy with more experience, I tried to give her some insight, to share a few words of encouragement and some of my own coping mechanisms.

"Hey, my man, you disagree?" Mia's friend said to the white guy. "He keeps shaking his head at everything Mr. Watkins is saying."

"Relax!" Mia said, hugging her friend. He pulled away.

"Nah, he shaking his neck like he having a seizure or something. I wanna know why!"

I laughed and said, "It's all good to me."

"I just feel like people talk about race too much, and I asked him a question about the Belvedere," the white guy said, pointing at me. "And he just blew me off like I was nothing! Ha! Like, what is that about?"

"Lesson one," I said. "Even though I answered your question, I really don't owe you an explanation. See, I'm too busy being oppressed to explain oppression to you."

"Nah, Watkins, explain it," Mia said.

"Nope, no worries, I'm just going to mind my business and pay my bill," said the white guy.

"But you put yourself in the conversation!" Mia replied. We all laughed. The white guy hung around for another fifteen minutes in silence then left.

"I didn't want that guy to leave," said Mia's friend. "I really want to know how he felt about race."

"I don't think he really wanted to talk about race," I said. "Because in my opinion, he's a racist and doesn't even know it."

This is common. There are a number of racist types floating around. Think of the guy who says "I'm not racist" every time he justifies mass incarceration and police murders. He doesn't identify as a racist because he talks to black people in public places; loves professional sports, like the NBA and NFL, which are dominated by black athletes; and is totally okay with black people until they bring up race or question his privilege. Then we have the "I Don't Know That I'm a Racist" racists. This is the guy who doesn't think he's a racist because he finds Beyoncé attractive, but jumps across the street so he won't have to walk past a group of black people. The guy who looks at the black guy in his office with a raised eyebrow every time he misplaces his own wallet. Both of these guys are different but just as dangerous as the "Proud Racist" racists. Think the guy who wears a Confederate flag T-shirt while twerking at a Donald Trump rally, but you never see them in diverse settings like the "I Don't Know That I'm a Racist," so let's focus on them for a second.

I see guys like the "I Don't Know That I'm a Racist" all the time. They start race conversations and then ask questions that they don't really want the answers to, or think they already have the answers to and just want to waste your time. No statistic, study, or hard evidence can shift their stance—they are knee-deep in tradition and strangled by their own perspective. I'm not against anyone who wants to spend their time enlightening people who aren't intellectually curious, but just consider that it's hard making racists acknowledge their own racism in a system where racism is okay.

I personally like my racism to be slam-dunked in my face, like Jordan from the foul line or Shaq in his twenties. I prefer Klan rallies, bright blue Trump 2016 or 2020 shirts, soggy "Make America Great Again" snapbacks, and dusty overalls held up by extra-large, extra-shiny Confederate flag buckles. Give me swastika face tattoos any day, as disgusting as they may be—at least that's honest. Knowing who's against and who's with me makes it easier to navigate American reality. These guys who lie and conceal their racism pose a more difficult roadblock on our way to equality—whatever that is.

※

WHAT BEING INTELLECTUALLY CURIOUS LOOKS LIKE

"Professor Watkins, you got a sec?" a student asked at the end of class as I shuffled ungraded papers into my book bag. "You don't seem patriotic at all, like not even a little. What's up with that?"

He was a boy-next-door type of white kid in a vintage Orioles cap and matching jersey. He doesn't really speak much in class, but his essays are really good.

"Why do you say that?" I asked.

"Because of the way you called Jefferson a 'dehumanizing slave-holder, better known as the godfather of black oppression!'" he said with a laugh. "I don't know. I feel like he did so much more."

"Oh, he did. But the way you interpret his legacy is a matter of perspective," I answered. "Recognizing how my ancestors were being treated under his dictatorship doesn't really make me want to rush out and praise his legacy. Think about it like this: What if you recently found out that player plastered on your shirt was a genius, but also a human-trafficking rapist? Would you proudly wear his jersey?"

"Of course not," he said. "But I'll always love my country."

I thought about his comments on my drive home. History is my first love. Most of my leisure reading involves the topics of slavery and Reconstruction, so I'm constantly thinking about the development of America and the role Africans played. Even after years of research and stacks of books, I'm still amazed at what enslaved and freed Africans accomplished in the world under the harshest of circumstances. By harsh, I mean being kidnapped, stripped of family and culture, having a foreign culture forced on them, and facing overwhelming degradation, beatings, torture, rape, and murder in a place where discrimination against black people was not only legal, it was celebrated.

But back to those accomplishments. The sacrifices and accomplishments made by African American historical leaders, from Frederick Douglass to Barack Obama, make me and many other Americans more than proud. And yet the idea of my being both black and a patriot danced around in my mind. It feels impossible. What does that even look like? Does it look like Ben Carson or one of those other Uncle Tom black Republicans who always side against black people. It was Carson who traveled to Ferguson, Missouri, during his presidential campaign and foolishly said, "I think a lot of people understood that [Michael Brown] had done bad things, but his body didn't have to be disrespected. I heard also that people need to learn how to respect authority," as reported by the *Washington Post*.

"Respect authority." Is that what being a black patriot is all about? No mention from Carson of the trigger-pulling officer Darren Wilson's use of the N-word or the racist rhetoric tossed around by the Ferguson police department. Carson popped back up in the media after the campaign during his first address as secretary of Housing and Urban Development in March 2017, calling slaves "immigrants," as if they volunteered to come to America for a better life. I don't think so. I struggle with the idea of black conservatives in general—mainly because they all make comments like Carson's. Some aren't as extreme, but they still sound like apologetic, subservient, weak cowards. To me, that's non-American.

I then think about people like Oprah, Jay-Z, Maya Angelou, Dave Chappelle, and all the other black innovators who I don't know personally but who have mentored me from a distance, and how their amazing success stories can take place only in America. Seeing their talents and witnessing their social mobility forces me to work hard in an effort to reach similar heights, and that makes the American Dream real for me.

Their achievements connect me to so many others who believe in that dream, making my relationship with the country a love-hate thing. I love the opportunity wrapped around all of those amazing come-up stories, but I hate the bloody history and the way women, people of color, and the LGBTQIA community are constantly discriminated against. And yet I acknowledge the progress we've made. It's complicated.

I received an email from my student later on that night requesting a conference to finish our conversation and go over his midterm grade. I set it up for the next day and sent him this passage from Frederick Douglass, published in *The North Star*:

> For two hundred and twenty-eight years has the colored man toiled over the soil of America, under a burning sun and a driver's lash—plowing, planting, reaping, that white men might roll in ease, their hands unhardened by labor, and their brows unmoistened by the waters of genial toil; and now that the moral sense of mankind is beginning to revolt at this system of foul treachery and cruel wrong, and is demanding its overthrow, the mean and cowardly oppressor is meditating plans to expel the colored man entirely from the country. Shame upon the guilty wretches that dare propose, and all that countenance such a proposition. We live here—have lived here—have a right to live here, and mean to live here.

We both showed up at my office five or so minutes early the next day.

"Professor Watkins, why'd you send that Douglass quote?" he asked.

I unlocked the door and we both walked into my office.

"Look at all of your awards and trophies," he said, pointing to my wall. "Even you have a great American story!"

"I do," I responded.

Then I explained what Frederick Douglass called "the Great Tradition," a theory that African slaves built this country, meaning that they should not be shipped to a different place after slavery ended and that they deserve to reap the benefits of everything that America has to offer.

"Reaping those benefits has been a rocky road," I explained. "From slavery to Jim Crow to the prison-industrial complex and all the other different types of discrimination that allowed— allow—these racist people and institutions to function."

The fact is, I feel like the first real American in my family. Yes, my parents and the grandparents I met were born here; however, I'm a part of the first generation in my family to travel, to receive a good education, to own property, to advance. And my good fortune feels tainted when I see so many black people who may never be able to have the same experience. That lack of opportunity, especially among the people who look like me, is what prohibits me and many other blacks from being flag-waving patriots.

ON MAKING AMERICA GREAT (AGAIN?)

Being from a place like Baltimore, you don't really meet Republicans or people that listen to country music. However, writing has kept me on the road and I'm learning that there may yet be hope for relations between the "Make America Great Again" people and non–Uncle Tom blacks. America may not be as divided as we think. I first caught wind of this at the Southwest Florida Reading Festival in Fort Myers.

I stopped by the barbershop to see Mike before heading south. Wall-to-wall people, as always. "Mike, can you fit me in?" I asked.

"You got an appointment, D. Watk?" he replied. "I don't care how much I like your book, follow the rules. And yeah, I read it."

"Whatever, man," I replied, making my way to the door. I was stopped by a couple of dudes who I always see in front of the shop.

"Yo, man, we gotta shake," one of them said, holding his hands in my direction and then yelling at Mike, "He can have my appointment, yo! Keep doing positive, Watk! I'll catch you later, Mike."

"Your lucky day, D.," Mike said. "You up in thirty minutes."

So I flopped in the chair and looked up Fort Myers.

I like to do my research on a place before I pull up, mainly for demographic checks. Once I made the joke that fifteen-dollar apples at Whole Foods all have different names, like exotic strains of weed, in Jonesboro, Arkansas, which didn't have a Whole Foods at the time, so it made zero sense to the audience and I got zero laughs. I'm not doing that again. So, Fort Myers, the county seat of Lee County, Florida, and one of the many places that Trump dominated in the 2016 election. I called my publicist.

"You sure they want me?" I asked. "You do know that this is a Trump town, right? And my Trump opinions are pretty well documented."

She laughed. "They'll love you, D. You'll sell a ton of books and have a great time."

Mike lined me up, I paid him, promised to download the appointment app, and exited the barber shop.

"Yo, Mike still in there?" said the kid who was with the guy who gave me his slot. "I don't normally go to Mike, but I need to get right."

"Yeah, bro," I said. "What's your name? I know you."

"Twizzle," he responded, giving me a pound. "Yo, I know you cool with FMG Dez. That's my peoples."

"Yeah! Dez my bro!" I said. "I heard your music! You the one, bro!"

I leaned on the wall and sparked a cig, and he started telling me about all of the music he was working on and how he was going to put Baltimore on the map. His energy gave me confidence, and the fact that he's a fellow East Baltimore guy and had love for my work meant the world to me.

"Cuz me and you are the same," I told him. "You just rap your stories over beats and I put mine in books."

He gave me another pound, and I told him that I wanted to do a story on his life as a Baltimore hip hop artist when I came back into town.

"That's why we love you, bro!" he said as we parted.

If the young homies in Baltimore love me, Trump town will be easy. I was off to Florida the next day.

Now, don't get it twisted. I have held countless events with all types of white people—all types of liberal white people, that is. Normally, the white people at my events eat organic food, love cardigans, own multiple pairs of Birkenstocks for the summer and winter, and have at least one dashiki. They march, protest, avoid gluten, and quote James Baldwin. I didn't see too many of those types of white people at the Fort Myers airport, or in the hotel lobby, or at the actual festival when I checked in for my morning event, but I wasn't too worried. The organizers were extremely nice, and they greeted me with open arms.

"Hey, Mr. Watkins," an organizer said. "We are doing something new this year. Instead of you going on alone, you'll be on a panel in conversation with Taya Kyle."

"Me and Taya Kyle? Okay."

I'd heard of Taya Kyle. And I'd seen her book, *American Wife*, at the top of the *New York Times* bestseller list. Everyone who saw the film *American Sniper*, based on the book by her late husband, Navy SEAL Chris Kyle, saw a portrayal of her life too.

We had never met, but I thought it would make for an interesting conversation.

I didn't get a chance to read her book on such short notice, but I did my homework. She's a white woman; I'm a black man. Her family is famously aligned with the military and celebrated by people in every inch of the country; I'm an ex–street guy celebrated in about three neighborhoods. She contributes to Fox News; I've never returned a call from Fox News and have made most of my appearances on CNN and MSNBC. Kyle endorsed Rick Perry for president; I wouldn't even let Rick Perry run my errands, let alone my country. The list of our differences goes on.

Kyle walked in, and apparently, she had done her homework too. After saying hello, she acknowledged the death of my brother and said that she hadn't gotten a chance to read my book yet as she also didn't know that we'd be sharing a panel. I said it was cool, and we put together a quick game plan. We were escorted to the stage by a black cop wearing a custom-woven gun belt—who was tickled to meet Taya Kyle and probably would've shot me if I had gotten too close.

The stage was close to the crowd, which was mostly white and dressed in American flag apparel. There were even a few "Make America Great Again" hats scattered around the audience full of Alex Jones clones with a few Kellyanne Conways sprinkled among them. Again, clearly not my crowd.

When we sat down around the table onstage, there was a copy of Taya's book on display, but no copy of mine. "Where's your book, D.?" she asked.

"I don't know, I guess they forgot it."

"You have to be ready, D.," she instructed. Then she took her book down so it wouldn't look like she was the only featured author. I told her she didn't have to, but she insisted.

The moderator opened with questions regarding writing about the loss of close family members, which spiraled into a conversation about love, family, and quality of life. Taya shared those human moments in her relationship with her husband, and I talked about the gems of wisdom I'd learned from the many people I'd lost. Suddenly her audience became my audience too because our stories were bigger than color, political endorsements, and ideologies. We were identifying those universal truths that connect us all. Yes, Taya Kyle and I might as well be from two different planets within the same country; however, we both know what it's like to lose the people who meant the world to us and how important it is to share those stories.

Taya Kyle was exceptionally skilled at explaining how to endure a tough loss, how to share an experience like hers with others and use that journey to empower yourself and others, and even how to learn to love again. That's what I try to do on the road in front of different audiences almost every week too.

I pulled the microphone close.

"You know, for most of our lives, people are telling us that we are so different," I said. "But at the core, I think we all want the same things, like happiness, success, love, and the ability to make our families proud. It's that simple.

"You can look at me and tell I'd never vote for a person like Trump, right?"

The crowd chuckled.

"So yeah, we have our differences. But I bet we all love ice cream!"

Everyone laughed again and clapped. Taya and I congratulated each other and made our way to the signing table. Her line wrapped around the block, and I had two people waiting without books.

"We wanted to get copies of your book," a round man in a red Trump hat said. "But the store said there was a mistake with the order."

I could've exploded, and maybe I did on the inside. But I'd learned a valuable lesson, one that is more important than book sales, about the power of proximity. So many people dislike those from other groups because they never spend time with them. I saw hardly any black faces during the event, which lasted a whole weekend. How can conservative white people possibly understand African American culture with media outlets like Fox News, TheBlaze, and Infowars as their only guides? They might not know any real black people.

I bet many of the people in that room heard my story and now have an expanded perspective, just as I gained a higher level of understanding by listening to Taya. I'll still never vote for a person like Donald Trump and couldn't care less about Fox News, but I'm willing to listen to people with different experiences in real interactions, people who care and are intellectually curious.

If we spent more time together, we would be better able to recognize our similarities, along with how connected we really are, and create a more meaningful shared American experience. So, yeah, there's hope.

BUT HOW DO WE GET THESE GROUPS TOGETHER?

"Can I buy a cig from you?" I said to a lean dude in a kid-sized leather jacket.

"You can just have one," he replied, pointing the box in my direction. I yanked a Camel out, he sparked it and continued up the path.

I really thought I quit smoking, but I needed a puff after the panel with Taya Kyle. The conversation wasn't too intense or heartbreaking, however, the booksellers had forgotten to order my books and the capitalist in me curled up and died over and over again every time I heard someone say, "I wanted your book so bad, but it wasn't available!" I know I said I'd learned a lot and it was worth it, but I wanted my money too.

A few of the hosts came over to comfort me. "I'm sorry, we'll make this right." Or, "Would you like some cake and punch?" I just kept telling them not to worry. What was I going to do? Flip out and cause a wild scene as one of the few black guys in the middle of a zillion white people?

As my cigarette burned out, a middle-aged white man walked up to me.

"Hey, you had some good stuff to say," he said. "I'm not buying your book, but the talk was nice."

"Thank you," I replied. He went on to ask me what I thought of Trump.

"I'm a new Republican, D.," he said. "And I just think that Trump is going to get our people—meaning yours and mine—back to work."

I thought about those phrases, "my people" and "your people," as if we both aren't Americans.

"You know, man, I don't like new people," I said. "I can't trust them. Meaning that you have to be a Republican for at least two years before I can listen to any of your right-wing opinions."

He took off his hat and used the brim to scratch his head. "I'm not following you, Mr. Watkins."

"It's simple," I told him. "I hate new. That means new Republicans, new Democrats, newly single people, newly married people, newly fit people, and basically anybody who just started anything."

He laughed. "Man, you are a silly one!"

I explained how silly he was for not understanding. Like a vegan who is only twenty-six hours into an animal-free diet telling me how to eat—while I'm holding a chicken wing. Wait at least two weeks before you start demonizing me. You can't judge on your first day.

"I never thought about it like that," he said. "But Trump is new, fresh, with great ideas on getting all of our people in America back to work. It's that simple."

He said it again, all of "our people."

"You do know I am an American, right? African American, but still an American."

"Okay, I see what you are doing. I didn't mean it like that," he said, putting both hands up in a pushback motion. I moved closer to him.

"Funny how they call me African American and you can," I said. "It's like the divide is permanent, right?"

He pondered for a second. "Well, I'm not one of those people who say that unhappy blacks should go home to Africa. I understand why people do, because if you are unhappy you do have a choice. But Trump gets that because he meets everyone, the blacks, the Asians, everyone."

A representative from the bookstore that organized the festival joined the conversation. "Mr. Watkins, I just brought over ten copies of *The Beast Side*. I'm so sorry about the mix-up with your other book. Please forgive us. I'm new at handling festival ordering."

"Oh, you're new, huh?" I asked. Trump-hat guy and I both started laughing, while the festival guy looked confused.

I told him that it was all good and asked for a second. I then walked to the side with the Trump fan.

"Man, I don't know you and you don't me, but, one, I can't just get up and move to Africa, just like you can't just get up and move to Europe, even though no one is ever going to tell you to do that," I said. "And two, Baldwin said that he loved America more than any other country in this world, and exactly for this reason, he insisted on the right to criticize it perpetually."

"And who is this Baldwin?" the guy asked.

I then told him that he is one of us—tapping him on the chest, and then myself. We built this country; we contributed to all of the innovation, art, culture, and definitely the infrastructure. There was no need for me to drag him for not knowing who James Baldwin was. Getting him to think outside of the trap that is his context and skin color felt more important.

"Have a good day, man. I gotta run," I told him. "But remember—we'll always have issues until you learn to see 'them' as 'us.' It's not easy. I work on it daily."

I asked myself the question, how do we get these groups together? Everyone isn't as friendly as me or on a book tour. I continued to wrestle with this question as I returned to Baltimore, still having no answer.

I jumped off the plane and into an Uber. While thumbing through apps, dozens of Twitter notifications bombarded my phone—I opened it to see that Twizzle had been murdered. Right in front of the barbershop where we met. I never had a chance to write about his music, just a memorial piece in the *City Paper*.

How can we ever get these groups together if my side is always dying?

PART 4
PROXIMITY

13

BE THE PERSON YOU
NEEDED GROWING UP

So you want to make a difference? I'm going to tell you how, and it's very simple. The secret is to spend a little bit of time and a whole lot of love—strategically.

"Hey, Mr. Watkins, thank you so much for coming out," a twentysomething white woman wearing a lot of flannel said to me as I spoke at her Ivy League school. She continued, "I'm just a white woman from Seattle. I'm a photographer, and I don't really understand all of these black issues but I want to help. Like, how can I make a difference?" She then shrugged and went on to say that she took amazing photos in Ferguson.

"You aren't powerless," I told her. "Instead of just taking photos of suffering people, pull one of them aside and teach them how to use your camera. Tell them what a DSLR is, and about aperture and f-stops. Expose them to something they've never heard of. Tell them that being an artist is a career option. Then you will be making a difference." Head nods and applause followed.

It baffles me that you can earn enrollment in one of the top schools in the country but still not know how to help people. That doesn't make any sense to me. Either you are silly, lying, or don't really want to help. Did someone have to hold your hand and tell you everything that you needed to gain admission? Or did your hunger for an elite education force you to figure it out? People fight for the things they really want.

Writing has now taken me to many cities, and I'm always confronted with "How can I help?"—not just from white people, but suburban blacks, hip liberal Asians, and many other ethnic groups. It doesn't matter what you look like or where you come from, everyone can skill share. Skill sharing is simply sharing your profession or skill set with someone else in order to expand his or her future possibilities. I didn't know any writers or professors when I was growing up, so now I'm in my neighborhood teaching writing. It is key to pulling us away from the muck of class and racial divides in our cities and can put a dent in crime, which could help end over-policing culture in general. Lack of exposure outside of their neighborhood keeps kids from poor communities tied to negative cycles.

I think about that lack of exposure and opportunity when I see the outrage from communities, liberals, and the media after a police murder. Sympathizers are quick to slap a victim's name on a timeline or T-shirt. But the question remains, how are these people really helping the situation? What skills did Freddie Gray have? What was he exposed to?

People are always showing up to the party late—after an innocent black person is murdered. Famous preachers, corny musicians, and politicians pop up every time a black kid is shot and leave after the camera crews disappear without offering any help to the surviving kids.

Collectively, we all need to move past the rhetoric and part-time victim support so that we can really find creative ways to unite and share a universal respect, love, and understanding for one another.

Accessibility is the first step toward racial and social progress. How many people can actually reach you? Do you help them when they do? Making a difference can't be a hobby and should never be taken lightly. There's no such thing as a day of service, this is life work. Be a mentor and attend events that are important to your mentee, offer positive reinforcement, share your connections, and help them gain access to the tools you didn't have. You have to be the person you needed growing up.

Goofy pundits like Sean Hannity, misinformed politicians, and most of the people outside of our communities get it twisted when they try to define our progress and work ethic. We are far from stupid and the opposite of lazy. Black people built this country and deserve a fair shake like everyone else. We flourish as much as every other race when given the same, and maybe even fewer, resources.

So, if you care and want to do something like that woman from Seattle who asked how she could help, please share a skill and be a mentor to someone.

RESULTS

My lane is writing books and articles as well as encouraging people to learn to think critically through gaining an interest in literature. I haven't been at it that long but it works on multiple levels. Let me explain how.

Remember Young Moose? The rapper constantly harassed and jailed by Officer Daniel Hersl. Moose's incarceration bothered me deeply. First, because Moose was a ridiculously talented rapper and had a bright career. And second, I knew this cop was a bigger crook than most believed. As mentioned, Hersl had previously cost the city hundreds of thousands of dollars in misconduct settlements. Meaning that us taxpayers were not only responsible for paying his salary, but we were also paying for the crimes he committed.

After my article was published, Moose's manager gave a copy of the article to the judge, who looked deeper into the case and later decided that Moose should not be in jail. He was released. I'm not saying that my article was the deciding factor, but I believe it helped his case a lot. A few days after the paper dropped, a Baltimore high school invited me to speak. I wasn't sure what I'd be speaking about, and then I stumbled across a news box stocked with the *City Paper*, featuring the article I'd written about Moose and Officer Hersl. I pulled over, grabbed a stack, and threw them in the passenger seat.

When I arrived to the class, I passed papers out to all of the students and teachers in attendance. The kids loved the rapper. Most of them glued their eyes to the article, soaking up every little detail. As they read, I introduced them to the reality of being a journalist and the power of telling your own story.

"I really never thought about the news," a kid said. "I need to write my book!"

I honestly believe many of the students that day walked away with an urgency to speak for themselves and now understood that their lives depended on it. The teacher confirmed my feelings through an email, text, and by inviting me back. And again, the new batch of students read and enjoyed it—that felt amazing.

Win-win-win.

* ✹ *

MY JOB IN THESE STREETS

"Feed time, homies! Line up!" yelled Deion, sweating like Pat Ewing in the fourth quarter over the scraped charcoal grill by the gate.

He'd packed it with little wings, salty turkey franks, and saltier turkey burgers on a ninety-plus-degree day down in Bocek Park.

It's a Sunday, so old heads like me, wearing Under Armour mixed with Nike Dri-FIT, tried to blend in with the high schoolers on the blacktop—the up-and-coming stars. For hours we threw crossovers, jump shots, and slurs at each other, always keeping it fun and peaceful. I lost the second game. Two is my max, so I hit the grill line.

"Yo, are these chicken or pigeon wings?" I asked.

"They from Aldi's, D. Watk!"

We all laughed and said definitely pigeon. I threw three on my plate, snatched a bottle of water from the cooler, and found a spot in the shade. Dub rolled up on me looking all urgent and uneasy.

"Yo, yo, lemme rap to you right quick, D."

I hopped up with my plate of wings and followed him toward the street. He's built like a refrigerator in a tank top and work boots. I remember when he was ripped like a protein-powder model, but this food, these little salty wings, makes us all fat and sick.

"What you want, Dub? I'm trying to eat!"

"Come here, lemme holler at you!"

He told me that he was proud of me being featured in the newspaper for something positive and how he and his mom hung the article with my picture up on their wall.

"Come walk me down the street, D." As I began to exit the park, Dub dug in his pocket and pulled out a folded letter.

"Yo, if you tell somebody, I'ma kill you, in real life," he aggressively whispered. Someone from the court asked if I had next, but I waved them off as we crossed the street.

"Yo, you sick or something, big fella? What's going on?"

He told me that he had been talking on the phone with his daughter in North Carolina at least once a week. She had the bright idea of them exchanging letters and had even sent the first one.

"So, what, you want me to help you write a letter?" I asked. "Isn't that personal?"

"Naw, D. I want you to read it for me. I don't know what she talking about. Don't tell nobody, man, I swear!"

He looked down at his boots and kicked the gravel. I wondered how a forty-five-year-old man could not know how to read.

I thought of Dexter Manley, the former Washington Redskin who graduated high school, spent four years at Oklahoma State, and made it to the pros all while being illiterate. His talents allowed him to be robbed of an education.

In a way, Dub is like Manley. Before he landed his city job, way back before his prison bit, Dub was an enforcer—the guy who beat up the guys who owed the kingpins money. Some debtors got dangled out of windows; others he'd run down until they were breathless and then grind the heel of his boot into their gum line. Reading wasn't a requirement for his job, and just like Manley, he made plenty of money.

We used to call his overhand right "the sleeper" because every dude that caught it went right to sleep. Dub didn't discriminate. He knocked out young guys, teenagers, old heads, dope fiends, student athletes, street guys, rappers, and church boys.

"Walk me to the store, man," I said. He followed me up Madison and down Curley. "So, do you want me to teach you how to read?"

He said no because he was too old. He'd gotten this far without reading and his brain doesn't work that well anymore.

"I got love for you, my brother, but your answer sounds like something that only a person who couldn't read would say! I'm not reading your letter unless you let me or someone else teach you. It'll be between us."

"Naw, man. I work and I'm out on the street, yo. I just wanna know what her letta say and maybe get one back. I'll pay you, but I ain't learnin' readin'. Shit borin' anyway."

✳

"Reading is boring" is a phrase I've been hearing at the beginning of each semester ever since I became an adjunct professor. I give them my soliloquy on why it was illegal for slaves to read and how easy it was for masters to control populations of people with limited thoughts—partially due to illiteracy. I would say, "Being smart and developing complex thoughts without reading is like trying to get The Rock's muscles without working out."

Then I assign cool books like Sister Souljah's *The Coldest Winter Ever*, Jay-Z's *Decoded*, Liza Jessie Peterson's *All Day*, Jason Reynolds's *Long Way Down*, and essays by me and other writers I think they would like. I also scour the internet for articles that speak directly to them. I believe that everyone would enjoy reading if they had the right material. Obtaining material that speaks to them would not only provide the foundation for the basic critical thinking skills needed to function, but also spark a greater interest in literature outside of the classroom.

As a kid, I was introduced to Mark Twain's *The Adventures*

of Tom Sawyer and *Adventures of Huckleberry Finn.* These types of books turned me off of literature. I came from a neighborhood with shoot-outs, dirt bikes, police raids, junkie fights, block parties, and hoop tournaments. Adventures happened every day. Today, I understand how great Mark Twain is, but as a kid Twain seemed corny. Huck Finn wasn't rocking Jordans and black characters were rare in Twain's books. So, it was easy for my friends and me to think that they weren't for us.

I wasn't hooked on books until I read Sister Souljah's *The Coldest Winter Ever.* I was twenty-five and laid up in the hospital with nothing on TV except *M*A*S*H* and *Mama's Family.* A young nurse who worked the night shift had this book stuck to her face. Even as she reset machines and documented information on her chart, she couldn't put the book down.

"What's that book about?" I asked. "Must be good, you ain't put it down yet."

"You'd like this," she replied, briefly pulling up her head and letting out a small laugh. "It's about thugs like you."

"You think I'm a thug? That's crazy!"

"I'm joking," she said. "But your friends are too loud and y'all all smell like a pound of weed. Anyway, get some rest, you don't sleep nearly enough."

She cut the light off and closed the door. When I woke up, the book was by my bedside. I read it in under two days. She was right. It was the fastest I'd ever read a book in my life. Who knew you could write books about the streets? I would've read this book ten times if it was assigned to me in high school.

The Coldest Winter Ever opened up my mind and led me to consume more and more books. My thoughts changed. I developed new ideas. I was forever transformed. Within months I went from being a guy who solved problems by breaking a bottle over someone's forehead to using solution-based thinking when resolving issues. It was as if reading instantly civilized me. It also made me acknowledge the need for culturally relevant material. Familiar information is less intimidating. And if it worked for me, I believe it can work for anybody.

＊✸＊

Dub and I spit sunflower seed shells on the way back to the court. I stopped and read the letter to him after he asked for the ten-thousandth time. She closed with, "Thank you for the extra cash. I can't believe I'm finally off to college. I love you. You'll always be a part of me and even though you weren't there in the beginning, I'm blessed to have you here now."

Dub paused and snatched the letter. He turned away and said, "Hol' up, D., I gotta go down here right quick, yo. I'll see you on the court."

"Yo, are you crying?" I asked. "That's enough of a reason to learn! Right?"

He continued down Curley Street without a response.

＊✸＊

For weeks after, I thought about Dub and his daughter, wondering what I could do. I had written essays that have been read by thousands. But most of my friends in Baltimore—where only 7 percent of African American males in the eighth grade can read on grade level—had never clicked on one. They celebrate my success but don't even know my work.

Initially, my essays were intended to raise awareness about the ills affiliated with the modern black experience by telling stories straight from my neighborhood. Outside of my neighborhood, people were responding to my work favorably and sharing their perspectives and ideas for change through tweets and emails. However, I knew that waiting for that influence to trickle down into my neighborhood wasn't going to fix our literacy problem.

I'm responsible for sharing the power of reading with as many low-income people as I can reach because reading saved me. My inability to reach everyone does not exempt me from making a conscious effort to push literacy every day in the streets, online, and in the schools.

Teachers, parents, and community leaders must use material that our students, who are often referred to as nontraditional readers, can relate to and, more importantly, encourage more people to write. If my story doesn't resonate with a segment of readers, someone else's will. I caught up with Dub at a '90s party a few months after he showed me the letter. Most of the guys from the court were present in their old-school Cross Colours jeans and Karl Kani sweats. Dub was fresh in Nautica, New Balance, and square frames, just like when I first met him back in the day.

"Yooooo, you look like a fat-ass Uncle Phil version of the Dub I knew in '96!" I yelled, giving him a pound and a hug. The same pigeon wings were being served with chips, a Subway platter, and a bunch of alcohol. I pulled Dub to the side and said, "Yo, I'm still down on that reading thing we rapped about if you want, man."

He inhaled four or five wings at a time and spit the bones out like shotgun shells.

"Homie, I ain't got the time. I gotta second job now so I'm sendin' my baby girl more college money. She the smart one and that's good enough for me!"

That was good enough for him, but not for me. I know that

literacy plays a key role in communication. Our crowded jails, the trash pigeon wings we eat by not paying attention to the label, the multiple police shootings, and the many racial divides in America in general are influenced by illiteracy. People not being able to talk to each other and share ideas leads to conflict. Dub's okay being one of the thirty-two million people in America who can't read, and I can't force him to because he's way bigger than me—but seeing people like Dub makes me want to do everything in my power to make reading cool. My work is to destroy that "Dub" mentality that's so common in my neighborhood and many other low-income areas across America.

The number of illiterate people in our country is criminal. The number of people who are aware of the literacy rate and choose to do nothing is even more criminal. Popularizing reading in a country where so many people think they hate books seems impossible. However, I believe that those of us who care can do it if we work together collectively and just take it one word, one sentence, one paragraph, and one book at a time.

HOW I FOUND MY PLACE INSIDE THE SCHOOL SYSTEM: MY OBLIGATION

"Yeahhhh, Mr. Watkins, you ever gonna write a book like dem essays?" a bug-eyed skinny kid asked me. He was shoving Flamin' Hot Cheetos in his mouth and standing over me as I checked Twitter.

"Yeah, Shorty," I said, tucking my phone in my pocket. "It's called *The Beast Side* and it drops in September, so get ready. I'm going to make sure every kid in your school has one. I don't know how, but I'm gonna do it."

Knowing about Dub's inability to read left me with a mission to try to reach young people so that they don't make the same mistakes we made. Getting to them while they are still in middle school, or even high school, could change the trajectory of their lives.

The skinny kid gave me a pound, leaving some of the dust from his Cheetos on my hand. I brushed it off on my jeans.

"I'm speaking to another class in a few, can you show me to this room?" I said, pointing to my phone.

"Yeah, Mr. Watkins," the kid replied, crunching more Cheetos and passing me the bag. I followed him up the hall.

"Yo, Mr. Watkins, can we take a picture together? Matter of fact, can I post to my IG? Can you follow my IG?"

"Yes, yes, and yes," I told him, knocking on the door.

"Watkins, you too early for this class! They be here in like ten minutes. Lemme hold your phone, I wanna show you my IG. It's really lit," he said.

I passed him my phone. He logged out of my account and into his. After following my feed, he showed me the images on his account: dirt bikes, hood pics, and videos of him hooping. He seemed really good.

"You think you can play ball, Shorty?"

"Don't talk trash, Watkins, 'cause I'll take you down to the gym!" he replied, laughing.

The teacher walked up to us. "Mr. Watkins, is he bothering you?" she asked.

"Nah, this is my little homie!"

He asked the teacher if he could sit in on my talk.

"Sure, as long as it's okay with your teacher," she said. "Bring me a note from her."

Before running down to get a permission slip, he stopped.

"Can you shout me out on the 'Gram or Twitter? I'm trying to get my follows up. You feel me?"

"I got you, Shorty," I replied. "Hurry back!"

2016

My books dropped and, lucky for me, teachers started reading them, loved them, and began sharing them with children who felt the same. They all wanted to teach them, but the school system wouldn't pay for either book, so I started GoFundMes and spent my own money to supply the teachers that wanted them.

Eventually, I ran out of money, hit a dry spell, and then PEN/Faulkner's Writers in Schools and Hooks for Books swept in. Both organizations purchased copies of my books and donated them to city schools in Baltimore and DC. The deal was for me to make classroom visits and teach workshops to every class that received books and the students would get to keep the books because they were being stolen from schools. I read this article in *Pacific Standard* that said kids who grow up with books in their lives tend to experience more academic achievement than kids who don't—even if nobody reads them.

"Name another time in history when young black kids from the street were excited about reading. Something special is happening, sir," I said to a young school system executive in a clean suit.

"I've been to almost every high school in the city," I continued. "The kids love it. They are seeing value in themselves, telling their own stories, and even stealing the books! None of these kids from East or West Baltimore are being transformed by *The Scarlet Letter* or stealing, let alone reading, *The Crucible*."

"I'm well aware of your work, Mr. Watkins," he said. "I first heard of your book in *Oprah* magazine."

"With all due respect," I said, "I've been going into schools way before that *O* mag mention."

It's crazy how you can work extra hard right under someone's nose—closer than their mustache, even—and they still don't know you exist.

"Mr. Watkins, you have my word," the exec said, locking eyes with me. "We want our students to read, and every ninth and tenth grader will have your books! I promise!"

He squeezed my hand until the bones shifted; it even puffed and turned red. My uncle had told me I should always trust a guy with a firm shake.

I left his office feeling great—inspired, even. I felt like the city was really changing for the better and our kids were finally going to embrace books.

I guess my uncle's theory was trash because that school system official never called or returned any of my phone calls. Maybe more pressing issues came up. Undeterred, I kept up my school visits, continued to raise money, donate books, spend my own money to donate more books, and work with organizations like Writers in Schools.

2017

Just before the start of the new school year, a few teachers relayed with excitement that the Baltimore City School System was considering both *The Beast Side* and *The Cook Up* for required reading for high school students. Mr. O., a popular young teacher who had been having some success using my and other Baltimore artists' work, was leading the charge. I joined in their excitement, but not too much, as I've heard this before. The difference this time is that the bulk of high schools were already using my books and essays. I've visited most of them multiple times now, and dozens of teachers keep me posted via weekly texts, social media messages, and emails of success stories: how they couldn't get some students to read anything until they discovered my books. I thought that maybe the administration finally understood the power of supporting a local writer who will do more than just write about Baltimore, but actually take the time to visit schools for free and engage with students.

Maybe?

"Sorry, D., they passed on your book," Mr. O. said. "They decided to double down on Shakespeare and some books the kids don't like. I'm sorry, man. I'll still use your book."

"It's all good," I replied, shaking my head, squeezing my phone hard enough to crack the screen. It didn't crack but it should've. "I ain't trippin', man, they always run away from good ideas."

I was definitely trippin'. I threw the phone after we hung up and, yeah, that cracked the screen.

I was not only upset at being snubbed, but that the school board had decided to double down on Shakespeare. They'd decided to double down on books that kids hate.

Upon receiving the news, I sat outside my car near my office and chain-smoked a pack of Newports. When I fished for another cigarette and came up empty, I went back inside and started reading my own book. I wrote some essays and headed home. My tank was a little past empty, so I pulled over into a gas station near a housing project where I used to play basketball as a kid.

"Yo, put fifty dollars on pump 3 and let me have a Black & Mild," I said to the attendant.

I put the nozzle in the tank and went to sit in my car. The clock said 3 AM.

Where does time go?

"Yo!" a guy screamed. "Yo!"

I turned around to see a short, bug-eyed guy in a hoodie with his forehead tilted down toward the ground and his right hand wrapped under his shirt near the waistline.

"Watkins?" he said. "Mr. Watkins, what you doin' out here, man?" He turned around and waved off another guy who was inching toward us.

"Yo, what's good?" I said. "Man, what's up?"

He took his hood off.

"I still remember when you came to my school. You everywhere now, man. You really made it out here. Just like you said."

I've made so many school visits that I honestly didn't recognize the kid. It was 3 AM and I had been up for two days straight reading, editing, and smoking the worst type of cigarettes.

The threads on his hoodie were unraveling. His shoes were tattered and dragging.

"My man, you okay?" I asked. "You need anything?"

He told me that he wasn't doing so well at home, he wasn't in school, and that he's flat broke. I walked to the ATM and yanked out $60, and gave him a five with the money tucked in my palm. Then I popped the trunk and gave him a few copies of *The Beast Side* and said, "Stay up, man, be safe."

He said the same and I pulled out.

As I rode home, I realized why he'd seemed so shocked to see me. He was possibly going to rob me until he realized that we had met before. And then I realized who he was: that kid who had asked me to follow his Instagram.

A school visit may have saved me from harm. And beyond me, those visits provided hope to a lot of young people, probably saving them and others in the process.

And that's a reason to ignore the bad decisions made by the administration, to continue to show love to every community, and to keep doing the work that counts.

I've visited that gas station two or three times since, looking for the kid. Although I haven't been able to catch him, when I do, I hope to help him get back in school.

In the meantime, I have no choice but to do whatever it takes to make reading cool, to do the work that counts.

14

THERE ARE NO SHORTCUTS TO CHANGE

**The Baltimore Uprising left the city with a ton of "changemakers in train-
ing" dying to use their energy to fight injustices everywhere.**

I was trying to finish my books and still doing a lot of freelance
writing centered around police shootings, as there seemed to be a
new one every week. However, Freddie Gray's death felt different,
not just because it happened in my hometown but because it woke
Baltimore up. It shined a light on poverty, how segregated the city
really is, and the ugliness that exists within our police department. As a result, so many new activists emerged—street dudes
and squares morphed into revolutionaries and freedom fighters,
dedicating their lives to making a difference. I'm reminded of
Donnie, who would hit my phone every morning around 9 AM.
Donnie was an ex–car wash attendant from the burbs.

One day he called at 7 AM.

"Yo, D.! Wake up, kid!" said Donnie. "Yo, we need you! Wear
all black and meet us on North Ave. in five minutes!"

The sound of him slamming the phone continued to ring in
my ear after he hung up. *This guy is crazy*, I thought. I'd just

poured some almond milk into my vegetarian coco crunch from the health-food store, and if you've ever had healthy cereal before, then you know that you have to hurry up and eat it because there's only a three-minute window before it starts to get soggy. Donnie called again.

"Yo! D.! Where you at?" he screamed into the receiver.

"Yo, stop yelling in my ear!" I replied, trying to eat some of the cereal before it became mush.

"Hurry up, man, and remember, wear all black! Everybody is wearing all black," he said in a softer tone. "We are going to meet up, pray, and then lie down in traffic in front of the beltway!"

Donnie hung up again before I could respond. By now, my cereal was completely soggy and nothing was left in the box but coco dust. Donnie had finally lost his mind. Why lay down in traffic? More importantly, why wear black? Isn't the street black? Don't you want to be seen?

Donnie called back. "D.! Where—"

"Shut up!" I yelled. "Listen, clown! What are you talking about and why you keep hanging up?"

"My bad, brother Watkins. These white people, they driving me crazy. I've been up organizing all night," he said. "You one of our black Baltimore leaders and we need you out there to stand with us in solidarity against the new youth jail they are planning to build."

I laughed and asked why in the world would a bunch of black people, dressed in black, and lying in traffic stop a youth jail from being built? That may have been the dumbest thing I'd ever heard in my life.

"No, Donnie! It's a dumb plan and that's the problem with you dudes in general, y'all don't think."

"What?" he asked. "How you write about the issues affecting us but can't ride with us on this mission? Man, you need to be out here with us! This how we hold black writers accountable."

"First of all, you can't hold anyone accountable," I told him. "And second, blocking traffic only hurts the oppressed, not oppressors!"

"Really?"

I presented two different scenarios. One involving a Walmart employee and the other a college professor like me. If a Walmart employee is driving to work on a highway and has to stop because protesters are blocking the only exit that will allow her to get to work, she could potentially lose her job. She'll have to call her boss to explain the situation. Who knows what type of response she'll get? Whatever it is, it likely will not be positive. Whereas a college professor, or someone with more freedom in their work arrangement, could send out an email explaining the small disturbance and go on to enjoy his or her day.

"People with money and power don't have to rush," I explained to him.

As we ended our conversation, Donnie was planning to attend the protest. On some level, I felt his pain. I know what it means to be young, angry, full of energy, and want instant results. The easiest thing to do is unite with other people who feel the same way you do. I also didn't want a new youth jail to be built; however, I wasn't participating in any quick fixes.

Activism isn't a hobby. It's not something that can be handled in a few protests or a day of service. There are protests after every police shooting that goes viral. But where are the results? Who was brought to justice? There are no shortcuts for real activists. Activism is life work that requires connecting with all types of people on various levels. To make a real difference, you have to commit yourself for the long-term. If you're not prepared to do that, then you should stay out of the way.

Donnie and the protesters laid in traffic that day. The event garnered some attention from a few local newspapers, TV stations, and a hipster crew filming a documentary. Meanwhile, the jail was built and Donnie isn't an activist anymore—that's the problem with modern protest. So many people react in the moment and then go home without doing anything strategic to solve the problems they're rallying against. Watching Donnie helped me to realize that change was going to take more than peaceful protesting.

Protests, the internet, and social media are great. I watched a video of a police officer named Arthur Williams whaling on a guy named Dashawn McGrier on Instagram. My friends and I posted and reposted the video to all of our social media accounts, and dude was suspended and resigned within three days. There is power in being able to widely spread injustices and sometimes that works. However, what do we do for the victims who don't go viral? The ones whose attacks aren't caught on video? How do we share their stories and find social and economic resources to help change their realities?

First, we must know who they are and we can't do that without getting into the streets. That's the only place to truly identify the issues and face them head-on.

EASY MONEY

You don't have to be on *Oprah* to make a difference, my friends and I do okay with limited resources. I once saw a group of kids in Cuba playing baseball without mitts, the bat looked worn and the bases tattered, busting at the seams. The lack of supplies did not stop them from having a great time. You see, they mastered the game with limited supplies, so if they ever make it to a place that has the equipment needed to match their talent they'll be better than everyone else. That's us, we are like those kids in Cuba.

Baltimore City is full of people who get little to no media coverage and have limited resources, but are still making serious waves. Two of my favorite changemakers are Erricka Bridgeford and Antonio "Tone" Cobia.

Baltimore's murder rate is no secret, the entire nation is aware of the problems that we have with gun violence. People always reference it, give commentary, and write think pieces about our issues, but most never really do anything. Famous people from Baltimore will yell, "You know I'm tough, I made it out of Baltimore!," while never coming back to help make positive changes. That is why Bridgeford and Tone are so important, and need to be tattooed on the narrative of good that exists within the city. They aren't famous, they aren't part of any big-time organizations, and have never been on *Oprah* (even though they should be), but they give us hope.

Bridgeford lost multiple family members to gun violence and instead of trashing the city, she organized multiple cease-fires that connect the suffering communities' activists, politicians, artists, and members of law enforcement. Her cease-fire events are some of the most beautiful days in Baltimore, mainly because they force everyone to come together in song, dance, fellowship, and prayer, all in the name of love, peace, and unity. Beyond the cease-fires, Bridgeford created the Sacred 7 ceremony. The purpose of the Sacred 7 is for citizens to meet after someone has been murdered at the place where they were killed at 7 PM and pour love into the space. Bridgeford believes these spaces are sacred and

I agree. The Sacred 7 hasn't been around that long, but I bet we will see positive long-term effects.

Tone is the scariest person in Baltimore without a gun. Why? Because when he sees you, he makes you work out and it hurts. It doesn't matter if you are at a family cookout, a nightclub, or the grocery store, when he sees you, he's going to make you do something to better yourself. He even caught me some weeks after a walk-altering leg surgery and forced me to do some toe raises on the good leg, while balancing the other with my crutch.

Tone struggled with his weight and felt it was affecting his health. He worked out but remained tired and sluggish and could not lose any weight, so he focused on eating a healthy diet and changed his life. The weight fell off as his confidence grew, sparking him to dedicate his life to providing that feeling for others.

Tone, also from DDH, became bothered by the amount of overweight people in our neighborhood, so he created Free Sweat. Again, it's not a big organization or a viral hashtag, it's Tone coming to the neighborhood, gathering people of all ages, and professionally training them for free. To date, he's given so many people who may not have had the money or confidence to join a gym a place where they can learn and grow and where wellness can become a reality for them too. Free Sweat brings out everybody, from the elderly and young athletes to overweight writers like me. It has truly made our neighborhood a better place.

It's that simple.

So simple that you can do it too. All it takes is a little bit of time and a whole lot of love.

It doesn't take a celebrity or a million-dollar budget to help people. The deeper I moved into media, big fancy functions, and television, the more I realized how easy it is to become disconnected. Gaining a platform in this era transfers into instant cred-itability. Creative people brand themselves as black saviors and then proceed to suck up resources from the less-affluent who truly want to help—blocking people like Erricka and Tone from receiving what they need to push their efforts to the next level.

Listen to people who aren't rich sometimes.

AM I MAKING A DIFFERENCE?: A CHECKLIST

If some of these methods don't work, or you don't understand, or my stories aren't translating, here's a checklist.

- ✔ Do I truly understand the community I'm trying to service? And have I ever actually been there?
- ✔ Am I setting goals based on growth?
- ✔ If I'm giving money, is it getting into the hands of the people who need it the most, or is it collecting dust in the bank account of some wealthy nonprofit?
- ✔ Am I using my position to help put people in a position to make money for themselves?
- ✔ Do I see the people I'd like to help as *them* or *we*?
- ✔ Do I love the people I'd like to help?

Ask yourself these questions. And if any of the answers are "no" or "I don't know," you need to readjust some things.

15

DON'T MAKE IT OUT, MAKE IT BETTER

"Can't wait to make it up outta here, I hate it around here," Bug said, nursing a half-cup of Hennessy. "It's nuttin' on the menu but death. Death and these stupid dope fiends."

I filled up my cup and listened. We were sitting on Ashland Avenue. It was a beautiful, seventy-five-degree winter day—the sun dipped into the clouds and kids ripped and ran in every direction.

"Being around here just make you worthless, bro," he said. "Like I probably won't even visit once I go."

Bug was about to start truck-driving school. When he finished, he figured he could get a good-paying job, leave East Baltimore, and move into one of those cookie-cutter, soccer mom neighborhoods in the burbs, with a Best Buy and Target in walking distance.

"We lost Bo, Bip, Rell, Lil Dunk, Rap, Wise, Little, Ronny, Kev, the President, and Lil Dre. Man, I hate Baldamore! We like the last ones left."

As kids, we were told to make it out of the hood. The hood is basically the worst place in the world, responsible for all of the trauma and pain that comes with being black. We aren't taught about the systems that create that pain, the racist cops, the black sellouts, the tax-based schools whose funding is directly connected to the jobs that don't want to hire us, and how those things contribute to the trauma that only guys like us can comprehend.

"Jay dead, Ceddie gone, we lost Nard, Ro," Bug said. He took a slow sip. "Remember Justin? Manny dead, Turbo, Rib, Cheese, Don Don, Wop, Teka, Lor Tay, Man Man, Bill, Twizzle, and Buff too."

We sat and reminisced to ourselves. I felt his pain, it was mine too. The coolest, the flyest, and the funniest dudes are all gone. A lot of us thirtysomethings from East Baltimore are walking around without any peers, we really lost whole sets of people.

"I know you feel me," Bug said, looking in my direction. "I know you feel me."

"I hear you, but I don't feel you," I replied.

I tried to explain to him that we needed guys like us around when we were coming up. At the time, I was in college and he was learning a trade, but we'd both almost lost our lives to the streets on numerous occasions. What if more professional dudes were present in our hood, telling us not to hustle and showing us how to get money legally? Would our section of the city be so bad? We have to be those guys.

I didn't know that I'd end up being a professor and a journalist and working in television. Many people thought that success would drag me out of my neighborhood, but instead it gave me more of a reason to be in East Baltimore. Now the young people can see, work with, and interact with me and then these professions can be their reality. They know killers and dealers, but now they know scholars and world travelers too.

"I used to think the idea was to leave the hood, bro," I said. "But now I'm thinking we need to buy it, fix our schools, and build our own community instead of sticking out like a sore thumb in someone else's. I ain't never leaving."

"Man, you crazy."

We agreed to disagree. But it was all love all the time. Bug made it halfway through truck-driver school before he was murdered a block away from where we had that conversation. I wish someone was around to guide that young dude who pulled the trigger. If there had been, Bug and a lot of other good dudes would still be here, and for that reason I will always work, support, fund, and be accessible to East Baltimore.

Success for me isn't about making it out, it's about making it better.

AFTERWORD

A SEAT AT THE TABLE?

Can see myself in presidential campaign dinners
But I'm passin' blunts around a bunch of gang members
When you're too hood to be in them Hollywood circles
And you're too rich to be in that hood that birthed you

—Nas, "Reach Out" (2012)

I'm at an interesting point in my career where I don't really belong anywhere. For me, it's either dry chicken and connecting with elites who have the power to further my career or amazing chicken and being back on my block. The point is, that wherever I am, I feel like I should be working instead.

I'll explain.

My friend Asia invited me to an event. Not as a date, but because I'm a journalist. Journalists usually don't get invited to anything, so I went.

I pulled up to the event about half an hour early.

I glanced through the car's driver's-side window as soft gowns and sharp suits poured into the venue. The women were regal and the men looked like they were born in dress clothes. I wondered if they'd know I had just tied my tie by watching the same YouTube tutorial I watch every time I need to tie a tie.

Wall-to-wall professionals, many of whom I've seen before— on TV. They sat me at a table where the conversation went like this: What do you do? What did your parents do? Are you a Que or a Kappa? I'm fifth-generation Harvard, how about you?

"I'm not."

Followed by: I accomplished this and that because I own this and this and this and that. Glasses chimed and accomplishments were traded and held high like trophies. I listened and cracked a smile before I went to the bathroom and never came back. They knew I was from the street; they smelled it, and they probably think that's where I belong. The event was a huge waste of time and energy. I should have been working.

Then my friend Tonya invited me to a house party.

I arrived half an hour early to see my cousin Ty being pulled off a bloody dude who was happy to get away. Ty and his half-closed eye greeted me in the courtyard.

Think of an all-black *Fight Club*. Ty was a chubby Brad Pitt.

"Yo, I just beat on Rome!" he screamed with every vein popping out of his neck.

"Why are you fighting, Ty?" I asked. "That should stop at age thirty."

"He called my mother fat!" Ty said. Others gathered around us in silence.

"But she is fat, and so are you," I replied. Ty put me in a headlock and we all went inside.

As the party got started, a mix of Black & Mild, Newport, and blunt smoke filled the room. In the haze, you could see red plastic Solo cups and the most amazing chicken you'll ever have—chicken so good that chickens would eat it. There were gallons of liquor and people dancing in every corner. To my

right, people were telling stories about street legends from the
'80s and '90s, the early 2000s conversation to my left. I've heard
them all before, over and over again.

"I'm surprised you down here," a cute, short girl said to me.
"I thought you'd be up in the Hamptons or something like
Obama and Diddy!"

I laughed. "Hamptons in the winter? Anyway, I live up the street."

She told me to stay still, gave me her cup, and blasted to the
middle of the room. Her song was on and she had to twerk. I
watched. My cousin went back outside to give the dude a rematch.
Most of the party followed. I set her cup on the table and went to
grab something out of my car that didn't exist because I knew I
wasn't coming back to the party. I pulled Ty's arm minutes before
the fight and told him to roll with me because it's not worth it. He
didn't listen. I kept it moving.

And that's exactly where I am. Not polished enough for the
media elite, and too polished to get drunk and watch my cousin
fight. Therefore, I should be working.

And if I do my job, my remaining friends and family will become the elite. That's lots of connections *and* amazing chicken.

THE MESSAGE

For starters, beyond race and class there's good people and bad
people. You'll never know where help is coming from—just try
to embrace and acknowledge it when you see it. I also learned
that meeting celebrities, famous thinkers, and public figures I really had a lot of respect for is a bad idea. I hate to say it, but the
bulk of them let me down and it's not their fault. We place them
on these pedestals, expecting them to be heroic figures and they
are regular, just like us, or they just want a seat at the table.

A seat at the table should never be solely about inclusion—being able to sit and chill with oppressors and learning how to be a little oppressor yourself is not what we want. A seat at the table should be about destroying that table, smashing it to a billion pieces and forcing it to be reconstructed with the intention of giving everybody a seat, not just you.

Year after year we see people eyeing these seats, and year after year we watch them elevate themselves, get lost in the fame, and then wonder why nothing changes.

The days of one black savior are over. Most of the people who identify as black leaders in the mainstream are too famous to directly interact with the people who need them the most. I learned to rethink what a leader is, what a mentor is, and how to be a valuable ally.

It's simple.

Appreciate the small wins, they mean a lot. There are so many underserved populations all over the country in need of your help! Sometimes something as simple as giving a person a ride to school or a clean shirt can change their life.

I get how protests disrupt with the intention of getting a message out, but we all must do more. We have to work at creating jobs, introducing new career paths, helping people with their resumes or teaching them a skill that they can use. Marching in someone's name is honorable and can lead to them being heard for a day, maybe some weeks, but teaching them a skill or introducing them to a new perspective can set them up for life—especially if you teach them to do the same for others.

I learned that you can't save everyone. Someone was trying to murder this kid I knew around his mom's way, so I moved him and his clothes to his grandma's house on the other side of town.

I took him to MVA four times so that he could get an ID, and then helped him enroll in community college. The ladies at the front office instantly took a liking to him and gave him a laptop to use for when classes started. I also got my friend who manages a restaurant to hire him the same week that school had started. The kid thanked me hourly on social media, calling me his real dad. A few weeks blew by and he never attended a class or showed up for work. I randomly saw him around his mom's way one day selling loose vials of heroin; he even offered me one before he realized who I was. I asked him about the job and school, and he told me that he'd start another day, because he had a lot going on. Another day turned into a year, but not really, because the following fall, he was murdered on the corner, right around his mom's way.

Some people will unfortunately fall through the cracks. I also learned that it's not my job to check the fake activist, argue with white people about whiteness or privilege, or prove that I'm blacker or more oppressed than anyone else because I'm from the street and they aren't. These things are unnecessary distractions from the work and a waste of time—every major movement in history was plagued by users and self-serving opportunists, so that's not new. Those evil people don't need any extra attention, they always fade out. My job is to help people, to do the work with the understanding that the greatest rewards lie within doing the work.

It's the feeling you get when you see your mentee make it to college and then walk across that stage, help your homie who just got out of jail find a job and reunite with his kids, or take troubled kids off the street and put them in GED or job-placement programs—and still answer their phone calls when they get thrown out of the program. You push them to re-enroll, swinging by the jail to deliver a message of hope to lifers, make college fun for everybody, and open your class up to the community members who want to learn but can't afford tuition.

It's inspiring young people to value their stories, coaching new writers, and putting them in the position to publish, get agents, and start their careers. It's donating furniture to beautify worn-out classrooms, helping teachers connect with students beyond the classroom, and being a role model. It's acknowledging your mistakes, learning from them, sharing those lessons, and just being a friend, a real one. This is how I live my life, every day. Sometimes I win and sometimes I lose, but I'm blessed to be able to try.

Most importantly, I learned that the work doesn't take millions of dollars or followers, just a little bit of time and a whole lot of love.

ACKNOWLEDGMENTS

To my inner circle, my heartbeats, Caron, Buck, Brandi, Aunt Robin and Uncle Jed, Aunt Trudy, Kevin, Tia, Kondwani Fidel, Darnell Baylor, and Devin Allen—I truly couldn't do this without y'all. I love you guys more than anything.

To my brother Devin, rest in power. Free my brother Tavon "Rose" Robinson! To my mom, Jeanie; my dad, Big Dwight, I love you, keep fighting; brother Trey; my big nephews Quintin and Kahlil. To my sister Moe, I love you and we are going to get through. To my brother Alan Nelson, we'll make it back; Nathan Corbett; and the rest of my family (too many to list), I thank you.

To my super-agent Barbara Poelle, Todd Hunter, Chelcee Johns, Dawn Davis, and the whole team at Simon & Schuster, thank you for believing in me.

To Jordan Hoffner, David Talbot, Sarah Hepola, Andrew O'Heir, the bosses Erin Keane and Lexie Clinton, and everyone at Salon.com for making me a better person and writer daily.

Thank you to my extended family: the Brace family, my nephew Lil Devin, keep shining—I'm so proud of you; Tariq Toure, Mumbles, Noah, Lor Nick, Young Moose, Aunt Sonja

Sohn, Wes Moore, Wil Hilton, the Homie Raggs Man, Mama KoKo Zauditu Selassie, Jason Reynolds, Mitch Jackson, Yahdon Israel, Taylor Branch, Chris Wilson, the whole Baltimore literary community, Tony Lewis Jr., "Free Tony Lewis!," Donald Stevenson you made the book! Cullen and the whole Red Emma's family, Dr. Ibram X. Kendi, Dovecote, Ed, Anne and the Ivy Bookshop, Toure, Mohamed Tall, Mama Koko, Zauditu Selassie, Eric Singer, Dr. Eric Rice, my sis Dr. Wendy Osefo, Lawrence Burney, Positive Tone, Wallace Lane, Erricka Bridgeford, Mr. O., Reggie Thomas, Baynard Woods, Tracy Sherrod, Nikki Giovanni the legend, Moe Hatten, Day Day, FMG Dez, FMG Dink, the whole FMG, Jamal Walker, Lil Man, Dre, Fly Tye, the whole Dunbar, Tyrel Ventura, Tabetha Wallace, Caleeb, Jada Pinkett, and Overbrook for giving me a shot, Krishan Trotman and Latoya Smith for always holding me down, Wayetu Moore, Jennifer Ogunsola, Sheri Booker, Linda Duggins, my brother Therman McG, Aaron Maybin, Nice Shot Kyle, Icy, iQuell, all of my teachers and students, Marion Winik, and the whole UB staff! Thank you!

RIP Famma, RIP Big Lo, RIP King Mike Carter, RIP Uncle Dick, RIP Erica Garner, RIP Dana, RIP Big Al, RIP Myeshia, RIP Cheese, RIP Corey, RIP Don Don, RIP Wop, RIP Fat But, RIP Hurk, RIP Rib, RIP DI, RIP Skola, RIP Nard, RIP Bip Allen Jr., RIP to everyone we lost.

Sending love to Bucktown, D&J, DDH, Chapel, Douglass, Latrobe and all the projects, and the whole Baltimore.

Most importantly, thank *you*.

WE SPEAK FOR OURSELVES
PLAYLIST

1. "Where I'm From," Jay-Z
2. "Street," G Herbo
3. "Jungle," H.E.R.
4. "FEAR.," Kendrick Lamar
5. "WTF Is Black Girl Magic?," Kondwani Fidel
6. "ES Tales," Jay Rock
7. "Focus," H.E.R.
8. "My Moment," Tee Grizzley
9. "Trust the Process," Jay Wyse
10. "Surviving the Times," Nas
11. "At Your Best (You Are Love)," Aaliyah
12. "1985," J. Cole
13. "Sleep Walkin," Mozzy
14. "U Don't Know," Jay-Z
15. "Gonna Love Me," Teyana Taylor
16. "4:44," Jay-Z
17. "Overdose," YoungBoy Never Broke Again
18. "Duckworth," Kendrick Lamar
19. "Smile," Jay-Z

20. "Redemption," Jay Rock
21. "Rose in Harlem," Teyana Taylor
22. "Marcy Me," Jay-Z
23. "Preach," YoungBoy Never Broke Again
24. "FMG Dez," Autobiographic
25. "If You Know You Know," Pusha-T
26. "Rap Memorial," Don Q
27. "Blue Laces 2," Nipsey Hussle
28. "The Lady in My Life," Michael Jackson
29. "First Day Out," Tee Grizzley
30. "The Prelude," Jay-Z
31. "Up," Dee Dave
32. "Win," Tee Grizzley
33. "One on One," Yo Gotti

ABOUT THE AUTHOR

D. Watkins is an editor at large for *Salon*. He is also a professor at the University of Baltimore and the founder of the Baltimore Writers Project. His work has been published in the *New York Times*, the *Guardian, Rolling Stone*, and other publications. Watkins is the author of the *New York Times* bestsellers *The Cook Up: A Crack Rock Memoir* and *The Beast Side: Living and Dying While Black in America*. He lives in East Baltimore.